UP FROM THE PROJECTS

Up from the Projects

Projects

An Autobiography

WALTER E. WILLIAMS

HOOVER INSTITUTION PRESS
Stanford University ◆ Stanford, California

THE HOOVER INSTITUTION ON WAR, REVOLUTION AND PEACE, *founded at Stanford University in 1919 by Herbert Hoover, who went on to become the thirty-first president of the United States, is an interdisciplinary research center for advanced study on domestic and international affairs. The views expressed in its publications are entirely those of the authors and do not necessarily reflect the views of the staff, officers, or Board of Overseers of the Hoover Institution.*

www.hoover.org

Hoover Institution Press Publication No. 600

Hoover Institution at Leland Stanford Junior University,
Stanford, California, 94305-6010

First printing 2010
18 17 16 15 14 13 12   10 9 8 7 6 5 4

Manufactured in the United States of America

The paper used in this publication meets the minimum Requirements of the American National Standard for Information Sciences—Permanence of Paper for Printed Library Materials, ANSI / NISO Z39.48-1992. ∞

Library of Congress Cataloging-in-Publication Data

Williams, Walter E. (Walter Edward), 1936–
Up from the projects : an autobiography / Walter E. Williams
    p.   cm.—(Hoover Institution Press publication ; no. 600)
Includes bibliographical references and index.
ISBN 978-0-8179-1254-3 (cloth : alk. paper)—
ISBN 978-0-8179-1255-0 (paper : alk. paper)—
ISBN 978-0-8179-1256-7 (e-book)
1. Williams, Walter E. (Walter Edward), 1936– . 2. Economists—Biography.
3. African American economists—Biography. 4. Journalists—Biography. 5. African American journalists—Biography. 6. College teachers—Biography. 7. African American college teachers—Biography.
HB119.A3 W55   2010   2011281451

To the Memory of Connie
and to Devyn, the dear daughter she gave me.

Contents

Preface

DESPITE NUMEROUS PAST SUGGESTIONS THAT I WRITE an autobiography, I have long resisted doing so. That's partly because I never thought autobiographies were important in the larger scheme of things. Also, partly because of the press of so many other commitments, I decided not to take the time.

What prompts me now is a combination of factors, not the least of which was the urging by my now-deceased wife of 48 years, Connie, and our daughter, Devyn. In her loving and polite way, Devyn advised that if an autobiography were in my plans at all, it should be written now lest it end up as a work of fiction. That's a nice way to communicate to one's father that at age 74, one's memory is not what it used to be and that prospects for improvement are not in the cards.

Dr. Thomas Sowell, my longtime friend and colleague, suggested another important reason for an autobiography: there has been considerable "publicness" to my life. What I've done, said, and written, and the positions I have taken challenging conventional wisdom, have angered and threatened the agendas of many people. I've always given little thought to the possibility of offending critics and contravening political correctness, and have called things as I have seen them. With so many "revisionist historians" around, it's worthwhile for me to set the record straight about my past and, in the process, discuss some of the *general* past, particularly as it relates to ordinary black people.

An autobiography permits me to talk about my life as it actually was, or as I recall it, as opposed to risking having someone else—friend or foe—make untruthful statements, wrong assumptions, and distortions. In that regard, I'm reminded of the angry response that former Secretary of Health Education and Welfare Patricia Roberts Harris wrote in response to Dr. Sowell's two-part series, "Blacker Than Thou," published in 1981 in *The Washington Post*. Assessing his criticisms of black civil rights leaders, Ms. Harris said, "People like Sowell and Williams are middle class. They don't know what it is to be poor." Nothing is wrong with being middle class.

But both Sowell and I were born into very poor families, as were most blacks who are now as old as we are. A reader of Patricia Harris's remarks would have had no reason or information to challenge her assertions that Sowell and Williams "don't know what poverty is."

While starting out poor, my life, like that of so many other Americans, both black and white, illustrates one of the many great things about our country: just because you know where a person ended up in life doesn't mean you know with any certainty where he began. Although I do not want to appear egotistical, neither am I a shrinking violet. I can say with considerable certainty that I have amassed achievements, earned income, and accumulated wealth to an extent that would have been unfathomable by my ancestors.

How did that happen? Because unlike so many other societies around the world, in this country one needn't start out at, or anywhere near, the top in order to eventually reach it. That's the kind of economic mobility that is the envy of the world. It helps explain why the number one destination of people around the world, if they could have their way, would be America.

This autobiography is not intended to be a complete, tell-all story of my life. Instead, I have tried to capture some of its highlights and turning points, and to contrast growing up black and poor in the 1940s and '50s to the same experience today.

CHAPTER ONE

Starting Out

FIVE YEARS OLD IS MY EARLIEST MEMORY; that was in 1941. My sister Catherine and I were sitting on a bench in the hallway of a somewhat-ornate building with high ceilings, and we marveled at a huge painting of three galloping white horses. While I can't say for certain, my best guess is that it was that of either the Philadelphia board of education at 21st and Parkway or the Andrew Hamilton Elementary School at 57th and Spruce Street. My mother was in the office, enrolling us in elementary school.

We lived in a lower-middle-class, mixed, but predominantly black neighborhood at 5565 Ludlow Street in West Philadelphia. The grade school nearest our house was Hoffman elementary, just a block or so away. My mother thought we'd receive a better education at Andrew Hamilton, which was in our district but six blocks away. Hoffman had a relatively large black student population. Hamilton had no black students but many Jews. School authorities therefore encouraged my mother to enroll us at Hoffman, because they thought we'd feel more comfortable there.

Mom argued that Hamilton was within our school district and insisted that we be enrolled *there*. She knew we were eligible to attend Hamilton, because its students included the daughter and son of a Jewish merchant, whose business and upstairs living quarters were located just around the corner from us, at 56th and Market Streets.

Mom was a forceful yet dignified woman who didn't easily take no for an answer. I don't know what she said or threatened, but that fall we attended Hamilton, I in the first grade and my sister in kindergarten.

Though we were the first black students to enroll at Hamilton, we encountered no racial problems. The teachers treated us nicely, and so did the students. I do remember bringing a note or some other notice home to my mother saying that I had been selected to play a part in a minstrel play. My mother told me that she wasn't going to give me permission to be in the play. Instead, she declared, they could put burnt cork on the face of one of the white children.

My years at Hamilton corresponded with those of World War II. On certain days, there would be paper drives to help the war effort. That's when many of Hamilton's students would go from house to house collecting old newspapers. The patriotic desire to defeat Hitler and Hideki Tojo was one of our incentives; but another was that the class with the highest pile of newspapers, stacked against the schoolyard fence, would be dismissed from classes early. While my class won some of the time, I didn't enjoy the early-dismissal treat. My mother's instructions were to go to school and come home with my sister, who was one year younger than I. As a result, when my class won the newspaper-collection prize, I spent time in the school library until my sister's class was dismissed.

My mother worked at least a couple of days a week as a domestic servant. During those days, children came home for lunch. Hamilton didn't have a lunchroom, as I recall. So on the days my mother worked, she'd leave baked beans, Spam, or some other canned goods on a floor-heater vent—so that we'd have a reasonably warm lunch. She forbade us to light the stove. I guess she feared that we might burn ourselves or set the house on fire.

Another of her instructions was to turn on the radio when we arrived home to eat lunch and leave for the return trip when the music started for the *Life Can Be Beautiful* soapbox serial—or perhaps it was the *Romance of Helen Trent*. That was our clock. An additional instruction was to remain in the house after school and do our homework until she came back from her job. I didn't always obey. My sister would tell on me, resulting in either cancelled privileges or a spanking.

When the house we rented was sold, we moved in temporarily with my uncle James Morgan, who lived at 5950 Callowhill Street, still in West Philadelphia but quite a ways from Hamilton. So the last half of my fifth-grade year and part of my sixth were spent attending Commodore Barry Elementary School. We were on the waiting list for an apartment in the Richard Allen Homes, a large housing project in North Philadelphia, where my grandmother resided with her retarded daughter. In close proximity, but in different parts of the project, lived two of my four aunts, along with their families. I completed the first half of the sixth grade—back then, grades were divided into A and B—at Spring Garden, an elementary school within the project. For the second half, I attended John Hancock elementary at 13th Street and Fairmont Avenue.

I've been lucky in a number of ways, not the least of which was to have a strong, demanding mother. My father played no role in raising my sister and me. I recall his visiting our house only once; I couldn't have been more than five or six years old. He and my mother had separated, and they divorced during my early teen years.

My mother never spoke much about their differences except to say that he gave her no financial assistance to help raise us. His mother, Lugenia Williams, was quite ashamed of his dereliction, and when we visited her, she'd always give my sister and me some change for spending money. She played "the numbers"—illegal but popular—and was quite lucky at it; so she might also have helped out my mother financially. For our birthdays, she would give my sister and me a dollar for each year, plus round-trip trolley car fare whenever we visited.

My mother took my father to court over child-support payments. I'm pretty sure that he paid something, but it wasn't very much and it wasn't for long. With those payments and a couple of days' work each week as a domestic servant, Mom could make do. During the war years, several of my aunts had jobs at the Sun shipyard. The pay was good, and I recall conversations in which my aunts tried to convince my mother that she could also work there and earn much more. My mother declined, declaring that she was going to stay home and raise her two children and that if she only had one slice of bread, she would cut it into three pieces.

My father ultimately moved to Los Angeles. Occasionally, we later found out, he'd "sneak" back to visit his mother—sneak because there was a bench warrant for his arrest for failure to pay child support. After he completely deserted us, our support came from welfare, called relief at that time, which we were alternately on and off. Because it was such a pittance, my mother continued to work occasionally as a domestic servant.

Life Back Then

What was it like to grow up poor? First of all, we didn't consider ourselves poor; in fact, being called poor was an insult. Unlike my future wife, we had proper meals and decent clothing, though sometimes I wore shoes with cardboard in them to cover a hole in the sole. My mother budgeted what little money she had very well. She even managed to take us on vacations to see relatives—on my father's side of the family—who lived in Queens in New York City.

Those relatives, Aunt Sally Hopwah and her Chinese husband, owned a dry cleaning establishment. They had three sons. We enjoyed playing with the boys and taking trips to the Coney Island amusement park and the nearby beaches. Sometimes we'd leave the Hopwahs, having spent a couple of weeks, to take a train to Ossining, up the Hudson River from New York City, to spend another couple of weeks with my mother's friends, Lottie and George Charity.

Ossining is particularly memorable because of the crabbing we did, using traps baited with either chicken entrails or whiting, which was a very cheap fish at the time. Ossining is also memorable for another reason: a very pretty and friendly girl who was my age lived down the street from the Charitys. I believe her name was Evelyn, and I had a ten-year-old's crush on her.

In Philadelphia, during my pre-teen years, the 5500 block of Ludlow Street was a mixed-race neighborhood but predominantly black ("Negro" in those days). The houses were well kept and crime virtually non-existent. Once in a while, there was talk of gang fights between two gangs in West Philadelphia known as the Tops and the Bottoms. We never witnessed the fights, but rumors about them carried a lot of currency.

There was mischief, and my sister and I were participants. On 56th Street, not far from our home, stood some duplex-type buildings with—in the rear—small, unfenced yards where people hung clothing out to dry. (This was in the early 1940s, when few if any people had clothes dryers.) My sister and I found much delight, en route from school, about six blocks from home, pulling laundry off the line and tossing it on the ground. After our mischief, we'd run away laughing. Doing that was even more fun when the housewife shouted at us from her window.

One day my sister and I were in our bedroom, probably doing homework or reading magazines. She heard a knock on the front door and looked down the steps as my mother opened it. My sister whispered, "That's that lady!" We both moved back from view, as if that would make a difference. The lady, who was white, was telling my mother about our misdeeds. I heard my mother apologize profusely, thank the lady, and promise her that it would never happen again.

I don't remember whether it was right away or after dinner, but my mother got out her hairbrush and whipped our butts. It was probably after dinner, because one of my mother's techniques was to first scold, lecture, and promise a whipping, and then let us suffer in contemplation of what was to come. Sometimes the whipping never came, but that night it did. The bottom line: we didn't even walk the same way from school for a long time.

My mother never graduated from high school. She was the oldest of seven children, and her mother took her out of high school to help care for her younger siblings. While she didn't finish her education, she had high academic aspirations for my sister and me. She introduced us to the Philadelphia library at 40th and Walnut Streets. I'm sure that by the time my sister and I were eight or nine, we had our own library cards. After our chores were done on Saturdays, instead of attending a movie, as many kids did, we'd walk the eighteen blocks from our house to the library and carry home four or five books to read during the week. We both became voracious readers.

In 1947, we moved into the Richard Allen project in North Philadelphia. My mother didn't like the idea, but there must have been no other alternatives. She said that few landlords were willing to rent to a single woman with two children. North Philadelphia wasn't as nice as West Philadelphia. It had a large black population that was much poorer and less cultured, as my mother put it. Since it was a housing project, with greater population density, there were many more children to play with, as well as swings, basketball courts, and a nearby baseball field. So I liked the Richard Allen Homes. My older cousin by three years, Carl Green, lived on the same street as my grandmother. We played and got into mischief together.

Back in the '40s the Homes were not what they were to become—a location known for drugs, killings, and nighttime sounds of gunfire. One of the most noticeable differences back then compared to today was the makeup of the resident families. Most of the children we played with, unlike my sister and I, lived with both parents. More than likely, there were other single-parent households but I can recall none. Fathers

North Philadelphia's Richard Allen housing project, our apartment building during much of my boyhood.

worked, and the mothers often did as well. The buildings and yards were well kept.

A typical Saturday chore for me and many other children was to sweep the hallway and landing on the floor of the building where our apartment was located. We lived at 810-F Warnock Place, on the third floor of one of the four-story buildings, so sweeping and cleaning entailed two landings and two sets of steps. The people who lived on the first floor were in charge of the outside steps and the pavement. In those days, the Richard Allen administration office would periodically send someone to make inspection visits to all apartments to ensure cleanliness and good repair. Graffiti and wanton property destruction were unthinkable. The closest thing to graffiti was the use of chalk to draw blocks on the pavement to play hopscotch.

Although there were occasional "rumbles," as fist fights were called, the complex was safe. During the summer, especially on hot and humid nights, many children as well as adults slept outside, either on balconies or in the yards of first-floor apartments. Diagonally from our apartment was a street lamp. When I went to bed, I'd often see older men seated around a card table quietly playing checkers, pinochle, or bid whist, while sipping beer. When I awoke at five or six o'clock in the morning, a few of them would still be there. They had no fear of assault. Many families never locked their doors until late at night, after everyone was home. When people visited, they'd simply knock on the door and let themselves in.

There were gangs and infrequent gang fights. Two of the North Philadelphia gangs I remember were the Saints and the Bucket of Blood. They sometimes fought but mostly with sticks, fists, and knives; occasionally you'd hear about the use of a homemade pistol called a "zip gun." The thing about the gang activity back then is that if you weren't in a gang, it was unlikely that you'd be bothered. That's in contrast with today, when innocent bystanders are often shot and killed in drive-by shootings.

In those days, there was a thriving business community on Poplar Street, which ran along the north side of the Richard Allen project. Grocery, drug, and clothing stores lined Poplar between 10th and 13th

Streets. They were mostly small, Jewish-owned stores, though several were owned by blacks. Most of the grocery stores had unattended stands set up outside for fruits and vegetables—with little concern about theft. Often customers would select their fruits or vegetables and take them into the store to be weighed and paid for.

A long block away, at Ninth and Girard Avenue, was an A&P supermarket where my cousin and I would take our wagons to earn money carting groceries home for customers. A little further away was Marshall Street, which had Jewish-owned stores of every type and merchants with street carts selling just about any vegetable or fruit one wanted to buy. One of the strategies used by my mother, grandmother, and aunts was to shop late in the evening, just before closing time. That's when the merchants would sell food items for reduced prices. We called that "Jewing them down," a term not considered racist back then, at least by the people who used it. A little further from our home were the thriving business centers along Ridge and Columbia Avenues and various blocks along 29th Street.

There was nothing particularly notable about a thriving business community in black neighborhoods, except that it would one day virtually disappear due to high crime and the 1960s riots. Such a disappearance had at least several results: in order to shop, today's poor residents must travel longer distances—often to suburban malls—and bear that expense; high crime costs reduce incentives for either a black or white business to locate in these neighborhoods, because the people who prey on the businesses are equal-opportunity thugs; if a business does locate in a high-crime area, it must pay for additional insurance and take other precautions, such as the purchase of iron roll-down bars.

Some supermarkets go even farther, hiring guards and placing no items near entrances and exits. And some stores deal with their customers from behind bulletproof plexiglass partitions. Yesteryear, such security measures were unknown. But now, to stay in business, an owner must accept higher security costs. Customers must contend with the results: increased prices and lower-quality merchandise and services reflect those costs.

The absence of shops and other businesses also reduces work opportunities for residents. One of my after-school and weekend jobs was to work at Sam Raboy's grocery store, between 12th and 13th on Poplar. I waited on customers, delivered orders, stocked shelves, and cleaned up. Other stores along Poplar hired other young people to do the same kind of work.

Junior High School

We lived in North Philadelphia one year before I was promoted to the seventh grade and the start of junior high school, called middle school these days. My home room teacher was black—Mrs. Viola Meekins; she also taught me English. Most other teachers at the Stoddart-Fleisher school were white. Having had most of my elementary school education at Andrew Hamilton, whose student body was middle class, I was academically far ahead of my peers at Stoddart-Fleisher, who came predominantly from poor families.

Being academically ahead was a plus for me but a minus as well. It was a plus because Mrs. Meekins and other teachers thought highly of me and gave me more accelerated work. I remember their compliments on my diction and grammar, and frequently calling on me for answers. Occasionally, I turned in sloppy work containing misspellings. When that happened, Mrs. Meekins would tear my two- or three-page composition into four parts and put a note on the top of one of them: "At least you could spell correctly. Rewrite." It didn't take long for me to be more careful.

She often asked me to do non-classroom chores when she was teaching a lesson far below my level. Sometimes she'd give me trolley fare to deliver papers for her to the board of education or take care of other school or personal business. Most of the time, I'd walk or run, because even though the board was located about sixteen blocks away, I could get to it on foot—and keep the trolley fare to buy something to eat.

The minus side of my being academically ahead of most of my peers surfaced in some of my classroom behavior. Mrs. Meekins was a stickler on grammar. Many of my fellow students were not at all smart, and I'd trick them into giving nonsense responses to her questions. For example, she would lead the class in the recitation of parts of speech: "a verb is a word that shows action or a state of being . . . an adjective is a word that modifies a noun . . . an adverb modifies a verb, adjective, or another adverb."

Sometimes she'd call on students to recite one of those definitions. One day, as she was doing that, a student seated next to me whispered, "What's a verb?" I told him to say that a verb is a word that shows action or a plate of beans. He repeated that aloud. As I laughed hysterically and the class joined in, Mrs. Meekins looked at the boy in shock. She gave me an angry look, knowing that I had provided the answer.

Classroom antics resulted in several detentions along with summons for my mother to come to school. Mrs. Meekins explained that she could send me to the board of education or have me do other chores for her and that I would handle those as well as she could. But she could not leave her classroom or even turn her back; if she did, I'd have the class in an uproar.

Consulting with my mother, Mrs. Payton, the school counselor, said that once I got the foolishness out of me, I was going to go places. She didn't say that in my presence. But in my adult life, after one of my accomplishments or another, my mother would remind me, "Your teachers always said that as soon as you got some of your foolishness out of you, you were going places."

One event reduced some of my classroom antics. Fridays were typically early-dismissal days, with classes ending at two thirty instead of the regular three thirty. I had recently acquired an after-school job at U-Needa-Hat millinery factory. Jack Friedman, its owner, expected me to be there around three o'clock on Fridays to deliver hats to various retail outlets throughout the city. One Friday, as a result of misbehavior, Mrs. Meekins kept me after school. I protested that I had a job to go to, but my pleas fell upon deaf ears. When I was finally excused I ran to 8th and Arch Streets, told Jack Friedman a lie about why I was late, and kept my job.

As a newly minted graduate
of junior high school.

First Real Job

Delivering hats and doing other odd jobs at U-Needa-Hat was both fun and profitable. I think I earned between fifty and seventy-five cents an hour. For a thirteen-year-old in the late 1940s, that was pretty good money. Plus, there were fringe benefits, such as when Mr. Friedman or his wife sent me to the Jewish delicatessen down the street to buy sandwiches, knishes, and pickles. They'd always buy some for me. What better way to a growing boy's heart than food? I was always hungry.

I worked most days of the week and sometimes Saturday or Sunday morning, particularly during the weeks before Easter, Christmas, and other holidays, when ladies' hat sales rose. Some days, I'd finish my chores with little to do before quitting time. On those occasions, when I was alone on the third floor, I would try sewing wire onto hat forms. I had watched seamstresses doing that.

The first several attempts were disasters. But in the succeeding weeks and months of fooling around with the electric sewing machines, I was able to sew wire on a hat form—not as fast as Friedman's experienced seamstresses, but almost as well.

On Saturdays and sometimes Sundays, particularly during the Easter, Christmas, or fall peak seasons, Mr. Friedman would ask me to work most of the day. If there were no deliveries to make, his son and I would press hats. That's a two-person operation. One stood in the front of a gas-heated machine that can be fitted with different dies in the shape of different hat styles. Both people held a dampened square of a material called buckram, which is used for hat foundations. The buckram would be stretched while the front person brought down the top part of the die with a foot lever. Then the lever was locked into place for a few minutes while the material dried into a hat form. I especially liked pressing hats, and the pay was better. Instead of the fifty cents an hour, I was paid the piece rate, which was a certain amount per dozen.

One Saturday during the rush season, Sam, Jack Friedman's son, was quite perturbed over two of his seamstresses not showing up to work. As a result, the shop was falling behind in filling hat orders. That's when I owned up to having fooled around with the sewing machines and volunteered to help out by sewing wire on the buckram hat forms. Surprised, he looked at Jack and then at me and said, "Let's see you do it." Within a few minutes, after offering a tip or two along the way, both Jack and Sam were satisfied with the skills I had picked up on my own. I'm sure I wasn't paid as much as the seamstresses, but I was happy with the additional money I earned and also with the many compliments I received. (Today it would border on lunacy to allow a thirteen- or fourteen-year-old near a power machine, much less to operate it.)

One summer week, preceding the fall rush, Mr. Friedman asked me to come in to work on Sunday. I told him that I couldn't because I was taking my girlfriend to Willow Grove Park, an amusement park just outside Philadelphia. Mr. Friedman, somewhat perturbed, asked me if it made much sense to stop earning money to go spend money? I gave his question some thought, and by the end of the week I sheepishly informed him that I'd be in to work on Sunday. That was the first among many other values I would learn from Jewish people for whom I worked.

I had found my U-Needa-Hat job through shining shoes after school and on weekends. My mother, a cautious worrier, didn't want me to shine shoes. It took Aunt Frances, my favorite aunt, to talk her into allowing me to accompany my cousin Carl when he set out to do that. Toting our shoeshine boxes, we'd walk from North Philadelphia to the city's downtown business district. Stopping in taverns, lunch counters, and stores along the way, I earned enough so that I did not have to ask my mother for entertainment money.

One of my regular stops was at U-Needa-Hat to shine Jack and Sam Friedman's shoes. On one visit, Jack asked if I wanted to deliver a package for him. From then on, leaving my shoeshine box in their shabby office while delivering packages became a more and more frequent event. One day, Jack suggested that I leave the shoeshine box at home and just show up after school to deliver packages and do odd jobs.

I worked for U-Needa-Hat for a couple of years. I lost the job because one of Jack's employees complained to the department of labor that he was in violation of child labor laws. When an official from the department interviewed me about my work, I, like most other people, thought they were acting in my interest to get me a higher wage. Not at all. Friedman's seamstresses weren't interested in my welfare. They found out that I was using the sewing machines after they went home and on Sundays, and they didn't like the competition.

Always a Job

I've forgotten just how Mr. Friedman told me I could no longer work for him. I was quite disappointed, but in those days, there were many ways a youngster could earn money. Among my numerous other childhood jobs were: getting up at daybreak and accompanying cousin Carl to caddy at Cobbs Creek Golf Club; taking the farm bus to pick blueberries in New Jersey; and working with a huckster peddling fruits and vegetables along the streets of North Philadelphia. As a peddler, I earned a commission based on the baskets sold. Other times my cousin and I would shovel snow from residential and business sidewalks. When worse came to worst, we would collect bottles and take them to the store to claim the deposit, or collect newspapers, rags, and metal and sell them to a junk shop.

Later, as a high school student, after school and during summers and on weekends, I worked as a busboy and dishwasher at several of Philadelphia's Horn & Hardart restaurants. Carl and I also delivered mail for the U.S. Postal Service over the Christmas holidays. During two Christmas seasons, I had an after-school and weekend job working at Sears, Roebuck's Roosevelt Boulevard mail-order department packing orders for shipment.

In addition, I had an after-school position at a small stockbrokerage, sweeping floors, delivering packages, and performing miscellaneous other chores. One day, when there wasn't much to do and I was talking with a salesman who'd befriended me, he said something along the lines of, "I could sell your people a shiny vacuum cleaner before I could sell them a share of stock." (Back then, "your people"—meaning blacks—wasn't considered an offensive remark.) He continued, "Shares of stock will do much more than a vacuum cleaner."

I've forgotten my response, but a few days later, I asked him what "stock" was. He explained that purchasing "shares" of it made you part-owner of a company. A bit later, I asked him how I could buy stock. He explained that I should look at a list he gave me and choose a company I liked, and he would make the transaction for me. One of the companies on the list was Pepsi-Cola. I loved Pepsi—didn't know one thing about the company, but the soda was one of my favorites. I told the salesman, whose name I've long forgotten, that I wanted to buy a share of Pepsi-Cola. He purchased one or maybe two shares of Pepsi out of my wages. And as I recall, I wasn't charged a commission; he must have paid it out of his pocket.

I didn't have the job for more than a year. But even then, at about age sixteen, I'd purchase additional shares of Pepsi every once in a while, until the price rose and it became too expensive. The little bit of money I had tied up in stock was inconsequential. But the larger benefit was that, as a teenager, I began reading the financial pages of the The Philadelphia Bulletin to keep track of how my stock was doing. In the process, I looked at other stocks and read some of the financial page articles, without much understanding but with a growing acquaintance with finance. Years later, I sold the Pepsi-Cola shares in exchange for some in the Wellington Mutual Fund.

By today's standards, my youthful employment opportunities might be seen as extraordinary. That was not the case in the 1940s and 1950s. In fact, as I've reported in some of my research, teenage unemployment among blacks was slightly *lower* than among whites, and black teens were more active in the labor force as well.* All of my classmates, friends, and acquaintances who wanted to work found jobs of one sort or another.

A supreme tragedy, in light of the great civil rights gains made by black people, is that the young kids who live in North Philadelphia today don't have the work opportunities that I had. Early work experiences not only provide the pride and self-confidence that comes from financial semi-independence but also teach youngsters attitudes and habits that will make them more valuable and successful workers in the future. That is especially important for young people who attend rotten schools and live in fatherless homes. If they're going to learn anything that will make them valuable workers, it will have to come through on-the-job training.

Speaking of financial independence, I had an experience that might easily be considered child abuse by today's standards. In addition to making a "contribution" toward household expenses, one of my obligations with my earnings was to pay for my school lunches. I often didn't husband my earnings well, however, recklessly spending much of them on weekend entertainment and other items. I developed the habit of asking my mother, by Thursday or Friday, for a loan to pay for school lunches. I always paid her back.

One week when I asked for a loan, she responded with a lecture that began, "When you were spending your money, didn't you know you needed school lunch money for the week?" Sheepishly, I answered yes,

---

* Joint Economic Committee, *Youth and Minority Unemployment*, 95th Cong., 1st sess. (1977): 10–11.

and I had an idea of what was coming next: her declaration that she wouldn't lend me the lunch money.

Hearing that, I thought she was the cruelest person on earth, and I hardly spoke to her for the next few days. Because I had no other sources for a loan, I came home from school starving on that Thursday and Friday. Looking back, the entire incident must have been hard on my mother: seeing one's child hungry could not have been pleasant. But I learned a lesson. That was the last time I squandered my school lunch money. I adopted the practice of putting it aside as soon as I got home with my weekly earnings.

Many years later, I related this story to my wife and asked whether we could have imposed the same harsh discipline on our daughter. Fortunately, the occasion never arose. But my wife thought it cruel of my mother and said she would never do anything like that. I'm not sure whether I would have had the stomach for it, either.

Our feelings about this matter make a point relevant to today. Parents nowadays, unlike their parents, don't have as much will or stomach to allow their children to suffer the consequences of irresponsible behavior. After all, a few days without lunch is unpleasant but by no means life-threatening, and it might teach a lesson.

High School

In 1951, I graduated from Stoddart-Fleisher and started my freshman year at Benjamin Franklin High School. Some classes there were far more academically challenging than those at Stoddart-Fleisher—most notably, algebra and geometry, in which I averaged about a C over five semesters. My overall grades weren't that great, either; they weren't bad, but very uneven. For example, some semesters I earned A's and B's, while in others, C's and D's were the pattern.

There was one instructor who liked me and had considerable influence on my life: Dr. Martin Rosenberg, who taught English. He was a dedicated teacher. He held what he called college tutorial classes twice a week at 8:00 A.M., an hour before regular classes began.

Students received no credit for taking Dr. Rosenberg's class. What they got instead was his willingness to impart extra training to those who demonstrated college potential. He drilled us on grammar. Our classroom work and homework consisted of correcting sentences and of learning and using vocabulary set forth in a book titled *College Placement Examination*.

Later in the day, I was also a student in Dr. Rosenberg's regular English class. There, in addition to English grammar, he assigned such classics as *Beowulf*, Shakespearean plays, *The Canterbury Tales*, and *King Arthur and the Knights of the Round Table*. He'd read passages from some of them aloud to the class. Obviously in love with the classics, he dramatized them as best he could to whet our appetites for literature.

Dr. Rosenberg held high and demanding aspirations for us. He said that we should always aim for the stars because if we failed, we'd fail in style.

Some of my classmates weren't that bright, and I exploited them to my glee. In class, Dr. Rosenberg would often ask students to identify errors in sentences—misplaced modifiers, wrong verb tenses, and the like—that he wrote on the blackboard. Since I was pretty good in English, some students would hurriedly ask me what the mistake was while the teacher had his back turned or was questioning someone else.

In one instance, I told a particularly dull boy to tell Dr. Rosenberg that the error in question was typographical. Without knowing either the actual grammatical error or the definition of "typographical," the student raised his hand to offer the answer I'd given him. Dr. Rosenberg hit the ceiling when he heard "typographical error," demanding, "What in the hell do you mean a typographical error? Do you see me using a typewriter?" The entire class fell out in riotous laughter. Then he caught on and asked the cowering student whether I told him to give that answer. The result: another time being chased home from school by an angry fellow student.

Once I suffered the full brunt of Dr. Rosenberg's anger and ridicule. He was again writing sentences on the blackboard and asking students to identify grammatical or spelling errors. If memory serves, the sentence this time was, "The criminal who've they have sentenced is sick."

The student called on "corrected" the sentence by saying that "who've" should be "who." Dr. Rosenberg was about to erase the sentence and continue when I raised my hand to say there was another error. He asked what it was. "Who," I said, should be replaced by "whom," because that word was the object of the verb "have sentenced."

Complimenting me on my alertness, Dr. Rosenberg turned to write another sentence. I said in a barely audible voice to the student sitting next to me, "Here I'm paying teachers to teach me, and I have to teach them." Dr. Rosenberg heard my remark. Exasperated by my past classroom conduct, he verbally laid me out, telling me that teaching me this material was like casting pearls before swine and that I'd never amount to anything. He made other comments, using what he often called fifty-dollar words, that I've since forgotten. After that dressing-down, I felt like two cents. Nowadays, the use of such straightforward honesty and harsh language by a teacher to a student would be unthinkable, particularly by a white teacher to a black student.

The scolding hurt, but in the eleventh grade it turned out to be my first real high school challenge—and one that served me well. A marked improvement resulted in both my conduct and schoolwork in Dr. Rosenberg's class as well as others. I ultimately improved so much that I was chosen to deliver the salutatorian address at graduation.

Looking back at myself at the time, I realize that I sorely needed the scolding and that Dr. Rosenberg probably chose the best way to administer it. He also had no hesitation in dressing down other students, also in a quite crude manner, employing words like "idiot" and "stupid" as well as mild profanities. But in my case, he used "big" words and flowery phrases from the literature that he knew I understood.

Benjamin Franklin High School had the lowest academic rating among Philadelphia high schools. My mother wanted me to attend Central High, which was at the top academically. She therefore spoke to either Benjamin Franklin's principal or guidance counselor about having me transferred. They told her that enrolling me in Central would be like putting a rabbit in a horse race. Given my behavior and attitude, they were right. I'm guessing that had I attended Central, I might not have graduated at all. The advice my mother received and

Dr. Rosenberg's scathing rebuke were well deserved and needed, and I benefited from both. At that point in my life, I was not a very serious student, and I wasn't living up to any of my mother's high academic expectations.

She wanted me to go to college, but that was the farthest thought from my mind. She aspired to much more for me than I did. I remember the time when I went home for lunch, bringing my eleventh-grade report card for my mother to sign, because it was well past the return date. As I was leaving to return to school, I tried to hurry her into signing, but she read the report carefully. The grades were: English III (D—despite my general proficiency in English), American History (D), Geometry (B), Physics (D), French (B), Physical Education (B), Health Education (A).

My mother was furious. She accompanied me back to school, scolding me along the way, telling me how I was wasting the sacrifices she was making. The conversation was not only unpleasant but also embarrassing; no kid wanted to be seen receiving a tongue-lashing from his mother.

She spoke to the teachers who gave me D grades. They explained that I did not turn in my homework on time, played around in class, and exhibited a poor attitude. She took away most of my privileges as punishment.

By that time, I had lost most of my interest in school. Some of my friends were talking about joining the Air Force, and I wanted to join as well. My mother told me that since I was under age, she would have to give permission, and she wasn't about to do so.

Despite my rough passage through high school, I graduated in January. It occasioned quite a celebration for my family, because I was the first member—at least on my mother's side, and I suspect on my father's as well—ever to achieve that level of education. Everyone was proud of me, especially my maternal grandmother, Katherine Morgan.

She had been reared in Newport News, Virginia, as a daughter of a former slave carpenter named Daniel Pettus. She worked most of her life as a domestic servant and completed only elementary school. The family that employed her vacationed somewhere in the Philadelphia area. During the time she spent there, she met James Morgan, fell in love with him, and didn't return to Newport News. Instead, they got married and started a family that ultimately consisted of five girls and two boys. I never knew my grandfather, who died before I was born.

I was Grandmother Katherine's favorite among her five grandchildren. She would often visit us and take me back home with her for the weekend; my mother, accompanied by my sister, would come to get me. When I was eight or nine, I'd make the trip by myself from West Philadelphia to North Philadelphia, where Grandmother lived, taking the El (the city's elevated subway line) and one trolley. I recall traveling by myself as a big adventure. My mother's only concern was that I look both ways before crossing the street.

I had no plans after high school, and I'm not sure whether they had even crossed my mind. College, even if I was interested, was out of the question for financial reasons. Moreover, given my immaturity, had I gone to college immediately after high school, it would have been a disaster. What happened instead probably had a lot to do with my future: my father no longer concealed his coming to town to visit his mother. That was because my sister and I were almost "of age," so he couldn't be prosecuted for non-support.

On one of my visits to my grandmother's house, my father happened to be in town. Initially, it was difficult to accept the fact that here *was* my father. But he was a smooth talker and put on a great front. I was impressed by his fine clothes, fancy car, and money. When we talked, he regaled me with stories about Los Angeles and offered me a paid trip to visit him as a graduation and birthday present. Much to my mother's dissatisfaction, I left by bus for Los Angeles that March, after my January graduation, to visit for about two months. Looking back, I'm sure she felt betrayed, though she never articulated it. She was the one who had made many sacrifices to raise us on her own; yet there I was taking off to spend a long time with a father who made no contribution to my upbringing.

Surprisingly, my father and I got along well. He had remarried. Claire, his new wife, and her sister, Louise Bobo, treated me very well, and we remain good friends to this day. I was impressed by Los Angeles, especially by how well the blacks I met were doing. They had cars and dressed well, and many owned their homes or lived in nice apartments. That was a far cry from the way my family or the other Philadelphia blacks I knew lived. It was going to be Los Angeles for me, and my father extended an invitation to return.

Looking back, one of the saddest periods for my mother must have been when my sister, age sixteen at the time, became pregnant with my nephew, Leonard. My mother had the highest of aspirations for us and was very disappointed and despondent over—not to mention ashamed of—my sister's behavior. I wasn't much comfort to her. Although I wasn't getting into any real trouble, I was in rebellious adolescence.

My mother was a proud, independent, and what some might call stubborn lady. She hardly ever associated with our neighbors, whom she probably considered less dignified and cultured than she. An excellent seamstress, she made most of her own clothing and most of my sister's as well. Despite her meager income, she and my sister were always, as she called it, "presentable."

Our neighbors considered my mother stuck-up. When my sister became pregnant, I'm sure my mother thought the neighbors were talking about her, and they probably were. Teenage and unwed pregnancy wasn't nearly as accepted back in those days as it is now.

Needless to say, or almost so, relations between my sister and mother became strained over the pregnancy. What made it worse is that my sister didn't cooperate much. The counselor at William Penn, the high school she attended, told my mother that she could continue school until she began "showing." The counselor said that after she gave birth, there would be opportunities to attend adult evening classes. Instead of taking those classes, my sister simply dropped out of school.

In September 1953, she gave birth. There had been discussions of putting the baby up for adoption, but my mother decided to make the baby a part of our family. So little Leonard came home from the hospital to live with us. Our Richard Allen project apartment had two bedrooms. I had a room to myself. My sister never had one. For a while, she shared the bed with my mother, and later she slept on the living room/dining room couch. When Leonard arrived, his crib was placed in my room, something I did not mind and even found enjoyable.

Contributing to strained relations between my mother and sister was the latter's attitude and laziness. She didn't always change her baby's diapers on time, and would wait until they were all soiled before going to our building's laundry room to wash them. She'd leave the house with the baby in my care or my mother's and stay out late or overnight. Finally, she left home—taking the baby—to live with a girlfriend named Zimmerman.

On that occasion, my mother asked me to go to the girl's house to determine whether my sister and the baby were there. I reported back that they were in fact there. My mother got a blanket, and she and I walked to the Zimmermans'. As I recall, my mother told Mrs. Zimmerman something like, "Catherine is underage, she's my responsibility, and whether she's coming with me or not, I'm taking the baby." My mother did just that, and my sister didn't leave with us.

My mother then took complete responsibility for Leonard. On the days she worked, my maternal grandmother, who lived down the street from us, babysat until I relieved her after school—and later on, after work. Sometimes the principal sitter would be my Aunt Francis, who also lived down the street. Raising Leonard became easier after 1958, when my mother remarried. Her new husband treated Leonard as if he were his son.

Even before they married, "Pops," as I called Mom's husband, was helpful to the whole family, taking us grocery shopping and picking up the tab for everything. Although I have no direct knowledge of this, I wouldn't be surprised to learn that he was also giving my mother financial assistance. He was a generous man.

Catherine worked at a sweater factory. She continued to live with her girlfriend, but later moved into her own apartment. It must have been a year or so before I found out where she lived and visited her once in a while. I was eventually able to negotiate a settlement of some of the differences between my mother and her, which enabled Catherine to visit occasionally to see her son. She seemed to be satisfied with her life. It involved working for the sweater factory during its busy season, being laid off and drawing unemployment compensation for about five months, and then returning to work at the factory. This routine continued for at least five years.

After that, Catherine went back to school and earned her General Equivalency Degree. Then she worked for the U.S. Postal Service until she was in her mid-to-late twenties. During the 1960s, when my wife, Connie, and I visited Philadelphia from our home in Los Angeles, we tried to talk her into coming out to stay with us to take advantage of the opportunities in California. She never took us up on the offer.

Instead, she decided to attend Cheney University in Pennsylvania, where she ultimately earned a BA degree in elementary education. Although she continued working for the Postal Service for a while, Catherine did move to Los Angeles in 1978, where she became an elementary school teacher. She continued teaching until she became eligible for retirement.

CHAPTER TWO

Rudderless and Drifting

A VERY ENJOYABLE TRIP TO CALIFORNIA included lots of sightseeing in Los Angeles as well as jaunts to San Francisco and Mexico. When
I returned, I found a job at Penn Dry Goods, a textile wholesaler located
at 10th and Filbert Streets in downtown Philadelphia. I learned how to
operate a double-folding and rolling machine.

Textile manufacturers sold wholesalers fabric in large rolls about
seventy-two inches wide and fifty, seventy-five, and one hundred yards
long. The large roll is placed on spindles at the bottom of the machine,
fed through several rollers, then folded in half onto a cardboard form
and rolled into a bolt. The machine operator determines the yardage,
usually about thirty. In little time, I became quite proficient at the job,
and could operate the machine faster than the several bosses and the
three or four other workers.

I worked at Penn for about a year and a half. When there wasn't
double folding and rolling to be done, I assisted in the shipping room
and performed other tasks. Payday was Friday, and it was always a big
day. In late afternoon, after all the work was completed for the week, the
bosses would treat us to delicatessen food, and some of my co-workers
would shoot craps as they shared sips of whiskey with me; every now
and then a couple of the bosses would join us. I never held the dice, but
I'd bet on the side. Most often, I either won or broke even, and never
lost over $10 or so.

The best way to describe this period of my life is to say that it consisted of drifting and incertitude as to what I wanted to do. A typical day was spent working. After work, I'd have dinner, then I'd often play basketball at the Richard Allen project's recreation center. I attended movies regularly or spent the evening hanging around with friends, mostly with my *best* friend, Leonard Shaw. Sometimes several of us would stand outside a state liquor store waiting to ask an adult, with an offer of a dollar bribe, to buy wine or beer for us.

Most of the time, the adult was an older brother of one of my friends. On several occasions, I got quite drunk—most memorably and humiliatingly at Lois Anderson's party, when I vomited on the family's brand-new sofa. The Andersons were good friends of mine, and I was embarrassed to show my face in their home for weeks. When I did, Mrs. Anderson was quite forgiving, though she gave me a lecture about drinking.

Approaching my nineteenth birthday, I bought my first car. Several months earlier, I had started visiting used-car dealers, and when I found a car I liked, the dealer gave me a form my mother could co-sign in order to finance the purchase after a small down payment. I was elated. But she, with little hesitation, said she would not co-sign. Then and for several days afterwards, my pleas fell on deaf ears. Looking back, she was probably right in her decision: I didn't inspire that much financial confidence. In addition, she never made purchases on credit and thought poorly of people in debt.

Nevertheless, I was determined to own a car. So I saved my money. I did extra work like caddying on weekends and put aside most of what was left over from my Penn Dry Goods pay after contributing to the house and taking in a movie now and then. In about five months, I saved what I recall to be about $350 to purchase outright a gray, 1947 Chevrolet fastback.

I drove home from the dealer and parked on 11th Street, just under our apartment window. Entering the apartment, trying to conceal my glee, I asked my mother to come look out the window. She asked, "Look at what?" I replied, "See that gray car down there?" She said, "What about it?" I said, "That's my car."

She looked at me, and I looked at her. I think she was proud of my accomplishment, because she told me that it was a nice car and hoped that I'd behave responsibly with it. Mom wasn't long on praise; she never was until much later in my life. But for me, the car was my message to her that I didn't need her help: I could do for myself. The purchase ended the grudge I held against her for not co-signing.

Owning a car seemed to make me more like the man of the house. In addition to all the fun I had with my vehicle, I used it to run errands for my mother and take her shopping. For the first time in my life, Mom was depending on *me* for something, and that made me feel good.

Ownership also brought me closer to my stepfather-to-be. He was a master mechanic at the army's Philadelphia Quartermaster Depot. On Saturdays, when he, his nephew, and a couple of other men worked on their cars, they worked on mine, too. In the process, I learned a lot about auto mechanics, so much so that for repairs other than those requiring specialized machinery—such as wheel balancing—I did virtually all of the maintenance on the cars I owned until well into the 1970s.

Auto mechanics wasn't all I learned from my stepfather. There were lessons in life, too. A memorable example of those occurred while working with my stepfather. One Saturday, he decided to replace the clutch on his car. He borrowed several tools from a friend. After he and I completed the job, he asked me to do him a favor: give the tools a good cleaning and return them to the owner. I asked him why I should clean them; after all, they were greasy and dirty when we borrowed them.

My stepfather replied, in a teaching tone of voice, "Whenever you borrow something, try to return it in just as good, or better, shape than you received it." That way, he explained, you'll always be a welcomed borrower. That was one of many wise lessons he taught me.

Although I continued to work at Penn Dry Goods and continued to drift, having a car made drifting more fun. As a result of an argument with one of the several Penn bosses, I threatened to quit. When I told a different boss, who I liked very much, of my intention to quit, I received another lesson from a Jewish merchant. He asked me whether I had another job to go to. I said no. He then said, "Before you quit a job, make sure you have someone else's floor to spit on." So I didn't quit until later that year, when I accepted my father's offer to come to Los Angeles to live with him and attend college.

To Los Angeles and College

My father and I drove back to Los Angeles together during the summer of 1956, and in September, I enrolled at Los Angeles City College as a full-time student, benefiting from a highly subsidized full-time tuition of $12 a semester. I was fascinated with college and all of my classes. I took seven that fall and six during the next semester. Other than C grades in French and physical anthropology, I earned A's and B's in all classes. Just about every Saturday morning found me studying at the Los Angeles Public Library downtown. I adopted the practice of completing term papers by mid-semester, long before the due date, a practice that continued through my entire college career.

Often I'd spend the entire day at the library, returning home in time to eat and occasionally take in an evening movie. When I went to the library on weekdays, I'd spend part of the time a few blocks away, at the Los Angeles County Superior Court, watching criminal trials; I was very interested in the law and a career in that field. For the very first time in my life, I thoroughly enjoyed studying and learning.

My father had divorced his second wife and remarried. I lived with him and his third wife. I got along well with her; but after a while, my father and I began to have difficulties. Precipitating some of them was a confrontation I had with him about his abandoning my mother, sister, and me. His stated reasons for doing so weren't at all satisfactory. He told me that he and my mother just didn't get along. Not getting along with my mother, I argued, should have had no bearing on his obligation to support his two children.

As a result, life with my father became quite unpleasant. I moved out and accepted an invitation to live with Claire, his second wife, and Louise, her sister, on Buckingham Road in a very nice section of West Los Angeles.

I continued attending Los Angeles City College, but decided to return to Philadelphia after the end of the spring semester. That summer of 1957, I sent my mother bus fare to enable her to visit Los Angeles with money earned from a part-time after-school job double folding and rolling at the House of Fabrics in downtown Los Angeles. She stayed in Los Angeles for a week or so, and thanks to the generous loan of either Claire's or Louise's car, we had fun sightseeing. Along with Sammy, a girl that I met recently and was beginning to fall in love with, we drove down to Tijuana for a day. A few days later, my mother and I boarded a bus for the three-day journey back to Philadelphia. Just before leaving, I gave Sammy a "friendship" ring.

Back to Philly

Shortly after I returned to Philadelphia, I landed a job with the Yellow Cab Company. Although I wanted to continue college, there was no way I could pay the close-to-$2,000 tuition at a Philadelphia college. I could, however, afford two night classes at Temple University. One was a European history class and the other was Algebra I. As I recall, I didn't work hard, and wound up with a C in the history class and an F in Algebra I. I wasn't dismissed—but I didn't attend Temple again the next semester.

I recall that period as one of considerable confusion about the rest of my life. I wanted to be back in Los Angeles attending college full time and back with Sammy. Part of that confusion painfully ended when Sammy sent me an envelope containing the friendship ring that I gave her. Heartbroken, I telephoned her to ask for an explanation. She told me that she thought I was a nice young man with my whole life ahead of me and that I should find someone my own age. (Sammy was three or four years older than I.) Remarkably, there had been no intimacy in our relationship other than passionate kissing and necking. In fact, although twenty-one years old, I hadn't yet been truly intimate with any girl—though when talking with other young men, I'd lie about my sexual experiences, as I suspect many of the other guys did.

My job with Yellow Cab was very important for my future. In February 1958, I met the young lady who was to become Mrs. Williams. My first work assignment was the 4:00 P.M. to midnight shift. Driving a taxi was very remunerative and fun as I learned the ins and outs of it. I don't remember just how much I earned between commission and tips, but I'm guessing it was at least $400 a month—only about $2,600 in today's dollars, but a substantial sum back then. Part of the reason for the good tips was because I could give passengers information on how to get whatever they wanted, whether it was gambling, after-hours joints and speakeasies, or prostitutes.

During those days, driving a taxi was not the risk that it is today. Often when I was assigned the midnight to 8:00 A.M. shift, I'd park at a taxi stand, take a nap, and be awakened by a customer or the taxi telephone, on a pole or a wall, with an assignment. A cabbie doing the same today might be deemed suicidal.

Several drivers and I became friends, and we'd routinely meet at the diner across the street from the taxi garage, at 3rd Street and Fairmont Avenue, to have coffee and a snack. On some Saturday nights, we'd meet, have a snack, then go to a speakeasy. Bars closed around midnight because of Pennsylvania's "blue laws." Often we were met at the diner by the girlfriends of several of the guys, and we'd head out to a party or speakeasy. I didn't have a steady girlfriend, though I did date now and then.

One of my driver pals, Charles, had just started dating a woman named Connie Taylor. One Saturday, around quitting time, he and I were at a taxi stand waiting for our 4:00 P.M. to midnight shift to end and turn in our taxis. Just as we were about to head to the garage, a fare got into Charles's taxi. As he pulled off, we agreed to meet at the diner to go out that evening.

I turned in my taxi and walked across the street to the diner to wait for the rest of our group to arrive. Connie was seated in a booth waiting for Charles. We had met previously when we all went to an after-hours joint together. I sat down across from her. I've forgotten the nature of our conversation, though it could have been about a book she was reading, but we hit it off quite well. Connie later told me that I was the only guy that she met who knew something about literature and philosophy; at that point, she was quite taken with the works of Kahlil Gibran. As my taxi buddies started to arrive, I wrote my telephone number down on a scrap of paper and told her to give me a call sometime. Years later, Connie told me how arrogant she thought that was: in that era, "respectable" girls did not call guys.

Connie did call me, however. She had a girlfriend, Mabel, whom she wanted to introduce to me. We met at Mabel's apartment, talked, drank, and were entertained by the dancing of two homosexuals, one of them Mabel's nephew. Several hours later, Connie asked me to give her a ride home. That started our friendship. Quite a few months later, Connie told me that seeing me talking to Mabel made her want me for herself.

Sometimes I would call Connie to invite her to go bowling with me and friends. Other times, we'd just sit and talk for hours on her porch at the house she shared with her sister, Leah. Although Connie was no longer dating Charles, she and I were just friends. During the summer of 1958, I quit working for Yellow Cab and drove to Los Angeles.

Trouble with the Law

Going to Los Angeles at that time was largely prompted by trouble I had gotten into with the Philadelphia police. In March 1958, I was arrested and charged with disorderly conduct, resisting arrest, and assault and battery on a police officer. The following circumstances led to the arrest: I was taking a passenger in my cab to the Reading Terminal train station. En route, I had to stop in the middle of a block of Pine Street in South Philadelphia, because a police officer was, for no apparent reason, standing in the street. Pine is a narrow thoroughfare, with cars often parked on both sides, so there was only one lane for traffic to move through. Becoming impatient, and with my passenger telling me he was going to miss his train, I shouted to the police officer: "Do you want me for something?" He made no reply, just looked at me. "If you don't want me," I shouted, "then how about standing aside and letting me drive by?" Still no response. I then shouted that as a taxpayer, I paid him to protect me, not to annoy me.

With that, the officer approached the cab with his hand on his pistol and opened the door, demanding that I get out and asking me who in the hell did I think I was talking to him that way. I attempted to get my passenger's name and address as a witness to the incident; but the officer warned him he'd better be on his way lest he be charged with interfering with a policeman.

The entire incident occurred right in front of a police station. I was pushed and shoved into the station, all the while protesting my arrest. The officer kneed me in the groin and punched me in the chest, and I was subsequently booked for disorderly conduct. Suffering painful cramps from the groin injury, I requested medical attention. I was taken to the nearby Pennsylvania Hospital emergency room and examined, and no injuries were found. Back in jail, I discovered that two additional charges had been filed: resisting arrest and assault and battery on a police officer. Their purpose: to provide the officer with a defense if I filed a complaint about his assaulting me. After spending the night in jail, I had a hearing in Magistrates' Court and was released upon posting a $500 bail bond.

While out on bail, I managed to secure appointments with Philadelphia Councilmen Tate and Alexander as well as an assistant district attorney to explain the situation and seek help. They told me there was nothing they could do. Fearful of being sentenced to prison, I decided to leave Philadelphia for Los Angeles and try to start my life again. I was surely indiscreet in mouthing off to the policeman, but being charged falsely with a felony was quite a shock. I had no prior police record. I later found out that the reason the officer was standing in the middle of Pine Street was that he was holding a parking spot for a fellow policeman who was preparing to back his private vehicle down the street, against the traffic!

In late May 1958, I set out for Los Angeles in my 1951 Mercury. Connie says that our first more-than-friendly kiss was the one that accompanied my goodbye. I stayed in Los Angeles with Louise Bobo, the sister of my father's second wife, and her young daughter. I explained to Louise the charges against me in Philadelphia and my plans to start a new life in Los Angeles. Louise thought I was making an unwise decision. She said that I'd be a fugitive and, if caught, there'd be dire consequences. She suggested that I return to Philadelphia, stand trial, and get the matter behind me.

Initially, I didn't think much of her advice. But after more conversation and a month or so of thought, I decided that Louise was right. Romantic feelings for Connie also played an important role in my decision; we had exchanged several letters during my stay in Los Angeles.

Shortly after my return, my mother married Thomas Burchett, her childhood sweetheart. He and my mother had been dating off and on since the early 1950s. He owned a three-story house in West Philadelphia. My mother, nephew, and I left the Richard Allen project. I lived in a small room on the third floor. I had an excellent relationship with my stepfather, whom I called Pops. He became the father I never had.

My day in court finally arrived in February 1959. The judge found me guilty of disorderly conduct and assault and battery on a police officer, and not guilty of resisting arrest. I was fined $75 and $25 in court costs. Given the light fine and no jail time for a serious charge, I'm sure that a councilman, congressman, or district attorney had spoken to the judge. And perhaps the judge had previous knowledge of police brutality; or perhaps he believed that my story was true (despite finding me guilty on two of the three counts). In my favor was the fact that I had no prior arrests.

All things considered, it was a good outcome, and I was and remain grateful for Louise Bobo's admonition to go back home and face the music. Nevertheless, I now had a police record that would have to be explained to future employers. That record would later cost me, as a college student, a part-time job at the Bank of America in Los Angeles.

Dating My Future Wife

After my return to Philadelphia, I was rehired by the Yellow Cab Company. Connie and I began steady dating—which back then was called going together. She introduced me to her very large family, and it turned out that they liked me a lot. Connie was the youngest of ten children. Her mother died shortly after her birth, and her father, who worked intermittently as a junk man, truck driver, and stevedore, raised his children with the assistance of his two older sons.

Connie had lived through the kind of poverty that was unknown to my family but typical in North Philadelphia. She actually went without meals and wore tattered clothing when she was young. During hard times, when her father didn't have rent money, he would move the family into a vacant house until they were discovered and had to find another place to live. She and sister Leah spent time in several foster homes and living with one relative or another—"living pillar to post," the common phrase ran.

I recall how proud I was to have Connie as my girlfriend. She was a very attractive woman, seemingly worldly and three years older than I. We became inseparable. Wherever Connie was, there was Walter, and vice versa. We'd attend concerts featuring Eugene Ormandy conducting the Philadelphia Orchestra at the Robin Hood Dell in Fairmont Park. Tickets were free, but you had to write away for them. Sometimes we'd simply show up at the Dell without tickets. I'd grab Connie's hand and drag her past the ticket collector. (She's never been quite as bold as I.)

Another of our favorite dates involved spending a day in New York City visiting museums and the evening taking in a live show at the Apollo Theater in Harlem. We'd drive up to the city and park the car in the vicinity of the New York Port Authority Terminal, leaving money in the glove compartment for the turnpike and tunnel tolls on the return trip. That way we wouldn't have to worry if we spent the rest of our money having fun.

Dating Connie led to another night in jail. It was a Saturday, and I had finished my four-to-midnight cab driving shift. Connie and I agreed to meet at her sister's house on 10th and French Street. She wanted me to get to know her oldest brother, Norman, who was visiting from Buffalo. Though she didn't know it in advance, Norman would be accompanied by a friend who had a romantic interest in Connie.

When I arrived, a party with loud music was underway. I hadn't been there for more than a half an hour when the police simply barged through the unlocked front door. "Bones," Connie's sister's husband, a big guy, grabbed one of the two policemen by the collar and threw him outside, demanding, "What in the fuck do you think you're doing walking into my house?" As that policeman and his partner stood outside on the pavement, Bones's huge German Shepherd barked and growled menacingly at them. The police called for backup, and in a few minutes several squad cars and a paddy wagon were on the scene.

When a policeman came to arrest me, I protested: "I just got here! What am I being arrested for? I haven't done anything." He replied, "You're being charged with frequenting a disorderly house." All the men, but no women, were loaded into the paddy wagon and carted off to jail. It turned out that when the police tried to arrest the women, Connie's older sister told the police that she was not going anywhere. She had eight children upstairs in bed and wasn't going to leave them. She said they would have to shoot her first. Connie's sister was a big woman, and her protest must have impressed the police, so the women stayed behind.

Spending a night in jail this time was fun. Four of us were placed in the same cell, and shortly thereafter, the police brought in three or four white guys and put them in an adjacent cell. As they were being escorted past us, Bones hollered, "I see they lock you honkies up, too!" That remark started an exchange of racial epithets between cells that lasted until everybody fell asleep. We all enjoyed it except the guy— dressed to the nines—who Connie's brother had brought to the party to meet her.

Next morning, we were all released without charges being brought against us. Although that was my second night in jail, it wouldn't be my last.

My mother, stepfather, and nephew liked Connie very much and for good reason: she was instantly likeable. She often had dinner at our house before we went out for the evening. But my mother did have rules. One evening, Connie and I were in my room upstairs, sitting on the floor talking and listening to Jackie Gleason music on my tape recorder. We both fell asleep, and when we awoke, it was around three in the morning. We quietly tiptoed downstairs, I drove her home, and I returned and went to bed. Next morning, when I arose and came downstairs, my mother said sharply, "If you can't take your company home at a respectable hour, don't bring them here." I tried to explain that we both accidentally fell asleep, which was indeed true, but I'm sure Mom didn't believe my story.

Sometimes when Connie and I were driving to one place or another, we'd pass the point where City Line Avenue intersects the Schuylkill Expressway (now Interstate 76). "One day," I'd say, "we're going to turn here and not stop until we reach Los Angeles." I would tell Connie about how well black people lived out there and about all the opportunities in California and my plans to return to and finish college. To her, that was just big talk, the kind she had heard from other guys. I learned later that Connie never believed me—and that her sister, Leah, had far greater confidence in my westward plans than she did.

I wanted a lot for myself—and for the two of us—and was willing to work for it. Since I had been to Los Angeles, I had confidence that I could make it there, but not the same confidence regarding Philadelphia. I thought I had much more on the ball than many of the well-to-do black folks that I met through my father in Los Angeles; if they could prosper, I could surely do so, too. But returning to Los Angeles with Connie would have to wait. In early 1959, I received notice that I was going to be drafted.

CHAPTER THREE

In the Army Now

IN AUGUST 1959, WHEN I WAS DRAFTED, my stepfather, a tech sergeant during World War II, told me that being in the Army is a million-
dollar experience that you wouldn't do again for a million dollars. That
was, I'd later learn, an understatement.

From Philadelphia, several of us inductees boarded a train for Columbia, South Carolina, to begin basic training at Fort Jackson. It was my
first time in the South. I'd been to still-segregated Washington, D.C.,
when I was very young; but I know that only because of the photos my
mother snapped and what she told us about segregation when she took
us to a theater. The cashier selling tickets displayed a sign reading "We
do not desire colored patronage."

Other than the standard harassment that a new recruit receives,
things for the most part went reasonably well for me at Fort Jackson. I
was made a squad leader early in the eight-week basic training program.
During the fourth or fifth week, I was politely relieved of that duty by a
specialist who told me that he wanted to give another soldier a chance at
the leadership position; in addition, he thought I needed a rest.

What really prompted his decision, I think, was a confrontation I
had with a white soldier in my squad. I had ordered the soldier to sweep
out the barracks in preparation for an inspection. He didn't like taking
orders from a Negro. We had words, and he shouted something to the
effect that he was from the town in Mississippi where "We took care of
Mack Parker." His reference was to the brutal and gruesome lynching,

earlier that same year, of Mack Charles Parker, a black man. After a few more exchanges of words, I offered him a "fair one," a term used in those days to refer to a fist fight. We never did fight. But the exchange was witnessed by one of the company sergeants, who probably told the specialist to relieve me of my squad-leader duties.

Basic training ended without further incidents, leaving me in the best physical condition of my entire life. I then had a two-week leave before reporting for my next assignment. I was very pleased with the transfer. It was to Fort Eustis, in Newport News, Virginia, only a four-hour drive from home. Connie and I discussed plans for weekend trips we'd take when I managed to get leave from the post. But before I had a chance to report to Fort Eustis, our plans went out the window, borne on a telegram I received while home on leave:

DISREGARD YOUR PRESENT ORDERS ASSIGNING YOU TO FORT EUSTIS, VIRGINIA. YOU WILL REPORT TO USA GARRISON (3190) FT. STEWART, GEORGIA. REPEAT REPORT TO USA GARRISON (3190) FT STEWART, GA. NOT LATER THAN 1700 HOURS 23 OCTOBER 1959. ORDERS BEING MAILED TO YOU.

Connie and I were heartbroken. Fort Stewart, in Hinesville, Georgia, was almost 700 miles away, so weekend visits home were out of the picture. But that disappointment figured small in the future that awaited me at Fort Stewart. The problems started before I set foot on base.

Into the Deep South

I left Philadelphia by bus the evening prior to my reporting date. It was the middle of the night when the bus pulled into Petersburg, Virginia. I was shocked to see, through the window, signs reading "Colored Waiting Room" and "White Waiting Room." Since there was no need for me to use the facility, I remained on the bus and fell back asleep. But I'd had my first adult encounter with segregation. I'm sure there were similar practices in South Carolina where Fort Jackson was located, but my only two trips off that base were to attend functions held at Benedict

College, a black institution. So I had not encountered discrimination South Carolina-style.

When the bus pulled into Savannah, I did have to use the segregated bathroom but not the lunch counter; my mother had prepared more than enough food for the trip, my favorites—fried chicken, potato salad, and pound cake—to last me for the trip. There was about an hour layover in Savannah. So I didn't return to my seat on the bus right away but instead walked around the block and smoked a cigarette. (I could have smoked on the bus: in 1959, people smoked just about anywhere.)

When the departure was announced and I returned to my seat behind the bus driver, I found an elderly white woman seated on the aisle side. I said, "Excuse me. May I get by?" In a very nasty manner she said, "I'm sorry, boy; this seat is taken!" I responded that I knew it was taken; it was my seat! After a few more exchanges, the bus driver came to my rescue telling the woman that "the boy" had had that window seat since boarding the bus in Philadelphia. She got up in quite a huff, loudly informing the bus driver that this kind of thing would have never happened back in her day.

The rest of the forty-mile ride to my destination was uneventful. But when I was standing on the steps, waiting for the bus to come to a complete stop at the Hinesville depot, I happened to glance at the woman who was my almost-seatmate, now seated several rows back. With a snarl on her face, she rolled her eyes at me. I stuck my tongue out at her. (I have no idea why I did that.) She opened the bus window and shouted to a sheriff, who happened to be right across the street, "Catch that nigger!"

The sheriff walked over to ask me what the matter was, of course with the salutation "boy." I told him the woman called him, not I. She replied, "The nigger stuck his tongue out at me!" Much to my relief, the sheriff started to laugh, and she angrily slammed her window shut. The sheriff asked me where I was going. He probably knew where, because even though I wasn't in uniform, I was carrying a military duffel bag. He got on his car radio and had Fort Stewart's MPs summoned to escort me to my new unit: H&S Company, 3rd Medium Tank Battalion (Patton), 32nd Armor.

Reporting In

"Private Williams reporting as ordered, sir," I said as I saluted Captain Elroy F. Smit, the commander of Headquarters & Supply (H&S) Company of my new battalion. I suspect that being accompanied by MPs didn't make a very good first impression. But in the weeks and months that followed, Captain Smit's first impression became the high point of our relationship.

Though the U.S. Army had been desegregated in 1948, through President Truman's Executive Order 9981, many black soldiers were being relegated to menial tasks such as grass cutting, sanitation, and KP ("kitchen police" duty). But quite a few were also assigned to the motor pool as mechanics and mechanic helpers, and a few had attained the rank of sergeant. The motor pool, my initial assignment at Fort Stewart, didn't work out well. I reported to a sergeant who told me that my job was to wash trucks and jeeps until a permanent assignment was made.

A few days later, when that sergeant saw me sitting and reading, he ordered me to paint a two-and-a-half-ton truck. I knew he meant paint the flat bed, but I asked, "The whole thing?" And he bellowed, "Yes!"

That was all I needed. I started painting the plastic rear window and then the tires. A crowd of soldiers gathered, laughing and shouting as they watched me. A lieutenant who approached to see what the ruckus was all about asked, "Soldier, what the *fuck* are you doing?"

I responded, in my best Southern Stepin Fetchit accent, "Boss, de sergeant told me to paint de whole truck; Ah's just doin' what he say." The lieutenant ordered me to get solvent and remove the paint from the windows and tires. Reporting to work the next day, my assignment was to wash trucks and jeeps. While no one was watching, I lifted the hoods of two trucks—a "deuce and a half" and a 4 × 4 utility vehicle—and used a powerful hose to wash the engine compartments, flooding the engines of both and rendering them inoperable. I guess I messed up the electrical equipment. Again, I played the stupid role, professing not to know what I was doing. To make the story short, I was finally ordered out of the motor pool and told to report to company headquarters for reassignment.

Looking happier than I was doing truck maintenance, my first job in Seoul, Korea.

For the next few days, I received such menial assignments as grass cutting around the barracks and cleanup details. Then I drew mess hall duty. The head cook assigned me to be the mop man. That was a pretty easy job. After mopping the floor in the kitchen and dining room after each meal, I could sit and wait until the next meal or until something on the floor needed cleaning up.

I believe it was my second day on that job when I decided to mop off the butcher block meat-chopping table. You'd have had to be there to appreciate the scene. Nasty, dirty-gray water was cascading over the sides of the meat table. One of the assistant cooks, a corporal who I liked, told me that the floor mop wasn't to be used on the meat-chopping table. But, he said, clean up the mess before the head cook came back, or he would be furious. I cleaned it up. Later that day, I mopped out the potato masher. The head cook saw me and went crazy. In very plain, vulgar terms, he told me to get out of his kitchen. I offered to clean the potato masher, but that only brought forth more vulgarity.

Elevated to Head Clerk

At roll call the next morning, the top sergeant dismissed the formation and told us to go to work. I told him that I didn't have a job, because the head cook told me not to come back to his kitchen. The sergeant, acknowledging that he'd heard that I "fucked up," told me to go to battalion headquarters to sweep and clean. I swept, cleaned, and ran errands there for several days—it might have been weeks—without incident. As it turned out, the head clerk of the battalion was completing his military hitch and would be discharged in a few weeks. I asked the sergeant major if I could have the job of head clerk. He almost laughed as he told me about all the qualifications necessary for the job: typing, answering the phone and taking messages, "cutting" military orders, etc. I'm sure he had been briefed about my previous conduct and was convinced that I wasn't up to that task—and maybe not to any others.

"Couldn't I even try?" I asked. Smirking, he said, "Okay, let's see what you can do." The head clerk agreed as they exchanged pitying glances with one another.

The head clerk gave me some transfer orders, several requisition forms, and some other materials. I typed them out expeditiously, correcting several misspellings and punctuation errors. I handed my work and the original documents, with my corrections underlined, to the sergeant when he returned to the office. As he examined the material, I could see the amazement on his face. He passed it on to the head clerk for his examination, and I went back to sweeping and cleaning.

Next day or a few days after that, the sergeant major told me that he'd try me out, and he assigned me to work as an understudy. For the next couple of weeks, I learned all the tasks assigned to a battalion head clerk, and I assumed his responsibilities when my mentor left to be discharged.

Becoming the battalion head clerk was never in my plans, no part of any brilliant strategy. It was sheer luck—because the clerk, sergeant major, and battalion commander were Northerners and perhaps sympathetic to me. I was the first black head clerk in the entire history of my battalion, and I liked the job. Doing it, I learned a lot about the military. The battalion was the convening authority for court-martial trials at Fort Stewart. As head clerk, one of my duties was to serve as court recorder. I prepared all of the trial records, and read and became quite knowledgeable about the Uniform Code of Military Justice (UCMJ). In fact, I became something of a resource person for officers who were assigned to prosecute or defend a soldier charged with an infraction. Learning the UCMJ and court procedure would stand me in good stead later on.

Fighting Segregation While Making Trouble

In those days, Fort Stewart held segregated dances at the post's service club annex—one particular night for black soldiers, another one for white soldiers. I persuaded some of the blacks to deliberately attend the dance on the "wrong" night. When about eight of us entered, people stopped dancing, but the music continued. After one black soldier asked a white girl to dance, the event was canceled. There was no disturbance other than some name-calling. The hostess called the MPs, and they made an "incident report."

Next morning, I was summoned by Captain Smit, who angrily threatened me with charges of inciting to riot. I told the captain that what we attended was a function on a military post and that my fellow soldiers and I were of the proper grades to attend. His manner softened a bit, and he said, "You know how it is down here." I knew what he meant, but I responded that I didn't know and asked him to explain. He didn't explain. I was excused. Smit didn't carry through with his threat of filing charges, but needless to say he was quite angry.

Fort Stewart's segregated dances produced another incident while I was there. At work, I received a call from one of the "line" company sergeants. (Our battalion encompassed the H&S Company and line companies A, B, C, and D.) The sergeant on the phone asked to speak to the sergeant-major. I responded that the sergeant-major was out and asked if I could take a message.

"Yes," the line sergeant replied, "tell the sergeant-major that I have plenty of nigger bus drivers but no nigger NCOs." He was referring to a procedure that sent a bus to town to bring local ladies to the service club annex. The sergeant felt at ease using the term "niggers" because he didn't know me and because before I became the battalion head clerk, there were no blacks in the administrative lines of communication. I responded, "Yes, sir," and left it at that, temporarily.

Several majors and colonels, all from Washington, D.C., accompanied the Army's inspector general on an inspection of Fort Stewart. They were being guided by our battalion commander, several other officers, and the sergeant-major. As a result, I was alone in battalion headquarters when the line sergeant telephoned. The inspection party returned to headquarters, and while its members were discussing their findings, I walked across the room to the water cooler. In a voice loud enough for all to hear, I told the sergeant-major, who was seated at his desk: "Sergeant So-and-So [I've forgotten his name] left a message asking me to tell you that he had plenty of nigger bus drivers but no nigger NCOs available to pick up the ladies for tonight's dance."

Instant silence followed. Then one of the officers in the inspector general's party roared, "Get that son of a bitch up here!" When the sergeant arrived, the officer, one of his colleagues, and the battalion commander took him into another room. I have no idea what was done or said, but I gave the sergeant a smile as he sheepishly left battalion headquarters.

A few weeks later, I sent a letter to the Department of the Army complaining about the segregated dances. I received no response, but the dances were later eliminated altogether.

Numerous forms of troublemaking made me unpopular with many of the soldiers, including black ones. Some warned that I was going to get into a lot of trouble, to which I'd flippantly reply, "What kind of trouble? Is somebody going to paint me black and send me to Georgia?"

Several black soldiers told me that black people were doing okay in the South, and it was Northern agitators like me who were causing them trouble. They told me that Southern blacks had their own businesses, homes, and churches. One added that blacks had had their own U.S. congressmen and senators. That to me was incredible. I told the soldier that he was crazy, that there never were any black congressmen and senators. When he offered to bet me $10, I gladly accepted.

In a week or so, he provided the evidence: Blanche K. Bruce, U.S. Senator from Mississippi, and several black members of the House of Representatives, including Richard Cain, Henry Cheatham, Robert Elliott, and Robert Smalls. I was dumbfounded. During my entire primary, secondary, and year-of-college education, I had never learned that several Southern blacks had served in the U.S. Congress.

While I was on speaking terms with most of the black soldiers, none of them except one—Lawrence Harvey—became a close friend. Harvey found my antics quite amusing, and he participated in a number of them. We did several unthinkable things that upset white soldiers and made black ones uncomfortable.

One antic had to do with television shows. "American Bandstand" was a soldier favorite. Along with other soldiers, Harvey would often be in the barracks dayroom watching the program when I entered after work. In loud conversation with him, I'd pretend that one of the white girls shown dancing was my girlfriend. Many of the soldiers knew I was from Philadelphia, where "American Bandstand" originated, and that might have added a bit of plausibility to my claim. At that time, blacks weren't allowed on the show, at least not in large numbers. But the girls I referred to were always white, and I'd tell Harvey, within full earshot of the other viewers, how this particular girl was cheating on me; I'd give him descriptions of our sexual activity, in the most vulgar and lewd terms.

The white soldiers, almost all from the South, did not find my comments amusing. The result was many verbal confrontations that one day turned into a fist fight between several whites and Harvey and me. We won the fight. But the company sergeant, after conducting an inquiry, accused me of instigating the trouble. I told him that I was exercising my freedom of speech. The white guys, I pointed out, were talking about the girls; why couldn't black guys do the same? The matter was resolved by the sergeant ordering that the dayroom television couldn't be turned on without a non-commissioned officer present.

I believe that one of the keys to my success in avoiding a court-martial for such pranks was that when I addressed a superior, the first words out of my mouth were always "Sir" or "In all due respect, sir"—even though the words were not supposed to be used with "non-coms." In addition, I honed the skill of making unimaginably ludicrous statements without the hint of a smile that might have revealed the delight I was suppressing. Most of the time, I imagine, the person I was addressing thought I actually believed what I was saying.

I'd always obey a command, although not always in the intended fashion. One time, our battalion was to participate in a St. Patrick's Day parade in, I believe, Savannah. I told the company sergeant that I had sympathy for neither St. Patrick nor Savannah and wished to be excused from the parade. He angrily huffed, "You will march in the parade!" Being the tallest man in H&S Company, I was in the so-called guide-on position; that's the spot to the front right of a formation, the one the others look to in order to maintain proper alignment and cadence. During practice sessions, I would march at the wrong cadence or even make the wrong turn, then apologize profusely for doing so. I did that in the practices for St. Patrick's Day and was excused from the parade.

There wasn't much the officers and non-coms could do about my behavior. I would be provocative and aggravating, but not enough for them to bring serious charges against me. Or so I thought. White soldiers did issue warnings that I not leave base to come to town. I heeded them; I wasn't about to become a victim of lynching.

Another method of aggravation I adopted was creating radio interference. The Southern whites among us liked to listen to country and western music on the radio. The sound could be heard throughout the barracks. I found both it and the accompanying sing-alongs distasteful. Above each of our bunks was a reading light, and I discovered that by unscrewing my bulb to the point where it flickered off and on, I could create static that interfered with radio reception.

Once the whites found out I was doing that, they came to my bunk to ask me to screw my bulb in. I offered a ludicrous reply, something like, "I like my bulb flickering off and on, and I don't appreciate the fact that a black person can't own something as small as a bulb without white people wanting to control it."

They'd go away cursing. I realized that if I hadn't been 6 feet 5 ½ inches tall, weighed 185 pounds, and won several fist fights in the company, they might well have gotten physical with me. Their solution instead: to steal my bulb, requiring me to carry a spare from the supply room each day. That back-and-forth routine persisted until the barracks sergeant negotiated a "peace deal": the white guys agreed to turn down the volume on their radios and leave my bulb alone; in return, I wouldn't create static.

By the way, when the sergeant asked me why I let the bulb flicker, I told him that it made me feel less homesick and hence less likely to go AWOL. He looked at me in astonishment.

There was yet another incident, and it must have aggravated the higher-ups. One Saturday afternoon, Lawrence Harvey and I were sitting on the barracks steps talking. In the course of our conversation, we realized that one of the sergeants was eavesdropping. We changed the subject and began conspiring to steal a tank, drive it to Savannah, and destroy the city. We livened up our fabrication by arguing whether a tank with a flamethrower or one with a ninety-millimeter cannon would be more effective, finally agreeing that a cannon would better suit our purposes.

Although neither the eavesdropping sergeant nor anyone else subsequently said anything to us about the "plot," Harvey and I did discover that we were being followed. We surmised that the sergeant reported our conversation to the commanding officer and that it was relayed to the Army's Criminal Investigation Division. Was the CID tailing us? We never found out.

Once we realized we were being followed, however, Harvey and I decided to have a bit *more* fun. Around 11:00 P.M., we would stroll by the motor pool, where the tanks were kept. We'd stand there for a few minutes, pointing at different tanks, then head back to the barracks to sleep. We did that several times. Neither of us was questioned by anyone, and we don't know when whoever was following us stopped doing so.

Thinking back on those days, I almost shudder at the thought of how reckless I was. But at twenty-three years of age, one doesn't think much about danger. It would have been a relatively easy matter for the people I'd antagonized to murder me and deposit my body in the nearby Okefenokee Swamp as food for alligators and crabs.

I'm sure that some of my troublemaking was inspired by the times. In 1960, a new phase of the civil rights movement was ushered in. It started with black college students conducting sit-ins at segregated lunch counters, the first being F. W. Woolworth's five-and-dime store in Greensboro, North Carolina. Students took their sit-ins not only to other lunch counters but also to segregated waiting rooms and government offices. Civil rights boycotts and picketing of segregated private and public facilities were becoming more common.

I did make official requests for reassignment out of the Deep South. On March 5, 1960, I submitted a "Personnel Action," Form 1049, which read in part:

> 1. UP [Under Provisions] of para 5d, AR 614, I request that I be granted a permanent change of station. If this request is granted, I feel that the armed forces would be benefited as well as myself in that there could be increased efficiency in the absence of the personal problem that exists as stipulated in the enclosure submitted as documentary evidence.

I request reassignment to Posts as follows in preference order: Fort
Dix, New Jersey; Philadelphia Quartermaster Depot; Aberdeen Proving
Grounds, Aberdeen, Maryland; and Fort Meade, Maryland.

The "documentary evidence" I submitted was a half-page reference to
the racial problems I had encountered at Fort Stewart. My request was
disapproved.

Court-Martialed

Although I was bad news for my assigned unit, H&S Company, at battalion headquarters where I worked, I was respected, if not liked, by the
headquarters personnel and the few others on the base with whom I had
dealings. That aspect of my reputation helped when Captain Smit, the
head of my assigned unit, managed to lodge serious charges against me,
and I was faced with a summary court-martial.

Here's what happened. One morning, Sergeant Bradford spotted
me during his tour of the barracks and ordered me to lay out a full field
display on my bunk. I've forgotten the prescribed way to do that, but it
involves laying out in a certain manner your helmet, mess kit, canteen,
and a bunch of other stuff the Army has issued to you. I went through the
drill. While I was waiting by my bunk for Sergeant Bradford to inspect
the display, another sergeant making the rounds of the barracks queried
me as to why I was still in the barracks and not at work. When I told
him why, he told me that he'd now seen it, so to put my gear back in my
locker and go to work. I did so.

During the lunch hour, I was summoned to see Captain Smit, who
asked why I hadn't laid out my gear for inspection. I told him that I did
lay it out and was told by another sergeant to put it all away and go to
work. (In the military, one is obliged to follow the last lawful command
by a superior officer or non-com.) Captain Smit called that sergeant into
the office and asked me to repeat my statement. The sergeant denied
even having seen me that morning. I protested that he was lying, but it
did no good.

For disobeying a direct command, I was subjected to a court-martial under UCMJ Article 91, which covers cases of failure to obey a lawful order or regulation. The text of the article reads:

(1) violates or fails to obey any lawful general order or regulation;

(2) having knowledge of any other lawful order issued by a member of the armed forces, which it is his duty to obey, fails to obey the order; or

(3) is derelict in the performance of his duties; shall be punished as a court-martial may direct.

The charges were drawn up (see page 51), and the court-martial proceeded. It featured me as my own defense council. (I had learned so much about the UCMJ, recording and filing court-martial reports, that I'd become quite knowledgeable.) I questioned both Captain Smit and Sergeant Bradford, focusing some of the questioning on whether I was a good soldier or not. Of course, they both declared that I was just about the worst they'd ever encountered.

My strategy with this line of questioning was to paint a sharp contrast between their opinion of me and the opinions of the officers who were trying me, were familiar with my work, and had from time to time sought my assistance and information in my capacity as battalion head clerk. To cap off my defense, I called my friend Lawrence Harvey as a witness. He testified that he had seen me lay out a full field display on the morning in question.

After about an hour or so of deliberation, the officers of the court found me not guilty of all charges and specifications (see page 52). When Captain Smit received the news, I was told, he was fit to be tied. It's humiliating for an officer to be upended by a private, and a black one at that.

When I reported to work the next day, the sergeant-major told me he was pleased at how things had worked out. He added with a laugh that he had a job for me: to type out the few notes of the court-martial that would comprise the official record of the trial proceedings; he noted

Charge   : Violation of the Uniform Code of Military Justice, Article 91

Specification

In that Pvt Walter E Williams, US 52 494 138, Hq Hq & Svc Co, 3d Med Tk Bn (Patton) 32d Armor, Fort Stewart, Georgia, having received a lawful order from 1st Sgt Elton R Bradford, Hq Hq & Svc Co, 3d Med Tk Bn (Patton) 32d Armor, his superior Non-Commissioned Officer, to lay out a full field display on his bunk, did at Fort Stewart, Georgia, on or about 2 April 1960, willfully disobey the same.

character, personally appeared the above-named accuser this 4TH day of APRIL 1960, and signed the foregoing charges and specifications under oath that he is a person subject to the Uniform Code of Military Justice, and that he either has personal knowledge of or has investigated the matters set forth therein, and that the same are true in fact, to the best of his knowledge and belief.

George E. O'Malley
SIGNATURE

Captain, Headquarters, 3d Medium Tank
Battalion (Patton) 32d Armor
GRADE AND ORGANIZATION OF OFFICER

Adjutant
OFFICIAL CHARACTER, AS ADJUTANT, SUMMARY COURT, ETC.
(MCM, 29e, and Article 30a and 136)

Officer administering oath must be a commissioned officer.

4 April 1960
DATE

I have this date, informed the accused of the charges against him (MCM, 32f(1)).

SIGNATURE Commanding Capt HHS Co, 3d Med Tk Bn (Patton) 32d Armor
GRADE AND ORGANIZATION

HEADQUARTERS, 3D MEDIUM TANK BATTALION (PATTON) 3D ARMOR, Fort Stewart, Ga 4 Apr 60
DESIGNATION OF COMMAND OF OFFICER EXERCISING   PLACE   DATE
SUMMARY COURT-MARTIAL JURISDICTION

1335
The sworn charges above were received at_____hours, this date (MCM, 33b).

FOR THE COMMANDER:

George E. O'Malley Captain, Adjutant
SIGNATURE, GRADE, AND OFFICIAL CAPACITY OF OFFICER SIGNING

1ST INDORSEMENT

HEADQUARTERS, 3D MEDIUM TANK BATTALION (PATTON) 3D ARMOR, Fort Stewart, Ga 4 Apr 60
DESIGNATION OF COMMAND OF CONVENING AUTHORITY   PLACE   DATE
Referred for trial to the SUMMARY court-martial appointed by Court-Martial

Appointing Order Number 12, this hqs, dtd 11 Feb 60

_____,_____19___, subject to the following instructions: 2 None.

BY ORDER OF LIEUTENANT COLONEL McNAMARA:
COMMAND OR ORDER

George E. O'Malley Captain, Adjutant
SIGNATURE, GRADE, AND OFFICIAL CAPACITY OF OFFICER SIGNING

I have served a copy hereof on each of the above-named accused, this_____day of _____, 19___.

SIGNATURE   GRADE AND ORGANIZATION OF TRIAL COUNSEL

1/ When an appropriate commander signs personally, inapplicable words are stricken out. 2/ Relative to proper in-

Source: In the author's possession.

☒ THE ACCUSED HAS NOT BEEN OFFERED PUNISHMENT UNDER ARTICLE 15 AS TO

GRADE AND ORGANIZATION OF OFFICER EXERCISING JURISDICTION UNDER ARTICLE 15	SIGNATURE
Capt, H&S Co, 3d Med Tk Bn (Patton) 32d Armor	*Geog T Smit*

RECORD OF TRIAL BY SUMMARY COURT-MARTIAL	CASE NUMBER **12** (Inserted by convening authority)

TO BE FILLED IN BY THE ACCUSED

I ☒ CONSENT ☐ OBJECT TO TRIAL BY SUMMARY COURT-MARTIAL

SIGNATURE OF ACCUSED *Walter E. Williams*

TO BE FILLED IN BY SUMMARY COURT IF APPLICABLE

When an accused has been permitted and has elected to refuse punishment under Article 15, trial by summary court-martial may proceed despite his objection.

1. THE ACCUSED, HAVING REFUSED TO CONSENT IN WRITING TO TRIAL BY SUMMARY COURT-MARTIAL AND NOT HAVING BEEN PERMITTED TO REFUSE PUNISHMENT UNDER ARTICLE 15, THE CHARGES ARE HEREWITH RETURNED TO THE CONVENING AUTHORITY.

GRADE AND ORGANIZATION OF SUMMARY COURT OFFICER	SIGNATURE

2. WAS THE ACCUSED ADVISED IN ACCORDANCE WITH PARAGRAPH 79d, MCM, 1951?   ☒ YES

SPECIFICATIONS AND CHARGES	PLEAS	FINDINGS	SENTENCE OR REMARKS
Specification and Charge	**Not Guilty**	**Not Guilty**	**None**
			NUMBER OF PREVIOUS CONVICTIONS CONSIDERED (MCM, 75b(2)) **None**

PLACE	DATE
Fort Stewart, Georgia	**5 April 1960**

GRADE, ORGANIZATION AND ARMED FORCE OF SUMMARY COURT OFFICER (MCM 4g)	SIGNATURE
1st Lt, Company B, 3d Medium Tank Battalion (Patton) 32d Armor	*Allen O Raymond*

Enter after signature, "Only officer present with command", if such is the case.

TO BE FILLED IN BY CONVENING AUTHORITY (MCM, 89, and app. 14a.)

ORGANIZATION	PLACE	DATE

ACTION OF CONVENING AUTHORITY

GRADE AND ORGANIZATION OF CONVENING AUTHORITY	SIGNATURE

ENTERED ON APPROPRIATE PERSONNEL RECORDS IN CASE OF CONVICTION. (MCM, 91c)

GRADE AND DESIGNATION OF OFFICER RESPONSIBLE FOR THE ACCUSED'S RECORDS	SIGNATURE

NOTE: Summary of evidence, if required by the convening or higher authority, will be attached on separate pages.

Source: In the author's possession.

that I would become probably the only soldier in military history to be both the subject and the official recorder of his own court-martial.

Less than a week later, I drew up papers bringing charges against Captain Smit under UCMJ Article 93, which covers cruelty and maltreatment and reads as follows:

> Any person subject to this chapter who is guilty of cruelty toward, or oppression or maltreatment of, any person subject to his orders shall be punished as a court-martial may direct.

I brought the statement of the charges to the battalion commander. He seemed very sympathetic, noting that I had been under considerable stress. The commander recommended that I take administrative leave, not charged as personal leave, go home and rest, and then, when I returned, consider any legal action against Captain Smit. It was a tempting alternative, and I took it. That was a mistake.

Ordered to Korea

When I reported back to the base after a couple of weeks of leave, the duty officer handed me a brown envelope with orders to depart immediately and report to the Oakland Army Terminal, some thirty days later, for shipment to South Korea. It turned out that during my leave of absence, strings had been pulled to get me out of Fort Stewart. An overseas tour of duty is 13 months, and I had exactly 13 months left in my two-year "active" military obligation. Normally, a soldier is not assigned overseas when the end date would be so close to his date of discharge. My particular assignment was to avoid embarrassment for the battalion and possibly trouble for Captain Smit.

Next day, I said my goodbyes to Harvey and drove back to Philadelphia. Both my mother and Connie were surprised to see me back home so soon again. My stepfather thought I had gone AWOL. He was convinced otherwise only when I showed him my orders.

Looking back, being shipped off to Korea might have been the best of outcomes, as opposed to my remaining in H&S Company and bringing charges against Smit. He would still have been my commanding officer, and chances are I would have been subject to some form of retaliation.

I was home for about thirty days. Connie and I were at this point deeply in love, and we had talked about marriage after I finished active duty. We decided to get married before I left for Korea. Since we were going to be married anyway, why not have her enjoy spousal military benefits such as PX privileges, medical care, and, as a "dependent," a monthly check. Because I was a private, not even private first class, the benefits were meager, but a lot better than nothing. More important in my own reasoning: I didn't want to risk losing Connie to another guy.

We were married on May 31, 1960, by the Rev. John Logan, minister of St. Simons, the Episcopal Church in which I was baptized and confirmed. Our honeymoon was modest. It consisted of several days in New York City, visiting places like Wall Street, the Statue of Liberty, and museums, and attending shows at the Apollo Theater. We couldn't have spent more than $200 altogether, but we had fun.

On June 5, I boarded a plane for the Oakland Army Terminal, and two days later, I was aboard a military troop ship bound for Inchon, South Korea. The unpleasant, nineteen-day voyage included a typhoon in the Yellow Sea. I couldn't get Connie off my mind. In addition, I was angry with myself for having been tricked into taking a leave of absence that allowed Captain Smit to avoid the charges I had prepared against him.

During the voyage to Inchon, a black soldier befriended me, and that helped allay some of my loneliness. When the ship docked at Pearl Harbor and the soldiers were granted shore liberty, he invited me to come ashore with him to have lunch with cousins who lived in Honolulu. I turned down his invitation and stayed on board, feeling depressed and sorry for myself. A week or so later, when we reached Yokohama, Japan, and were again granted liberty, I did accept his invitation to go ashore and do some sightseeing. Along the way, we stopped in a bar for beer.

The bar turned out to double as a house of prostitution. My friend hired one of the girls, and I was to stand by while he had his fun. As I waited, sipping beer, a Japanese girl grabbed my hand and invited me to accompany her. I declined—and later found out that he had purchased her services for me for a carton of Salem cigarettes that he'd bought (very cheaply) at the PX.

My time in South Korea was nowhere near as difficult as it had been in Georgia, but I still caused trouble. It started a few hours after landing in Inchon—on LSTs that ferried soldiers from the troop carrier to shore, passing other LSTs ferrying to the ship soldiers who had completed their tour of duty. We had been told to fill out forms that contained vital personal information such as blood type, race, religion, next of kin, etc. Disembarking soldiers were lined up in front of several Quonset huts, where warrant officers were inspecting the forms and handing out instructions for shipment to our assigned units.

One question on the form concerned race, and I had checked off "Caucasian." A warrant officer told me I had made a mistake. I told him that I hadn't made a mistake, that I was in fact Caucasian. We had a couple of exchanges: "No, you're not"; "Yes, I am." He wanted to know why I would say Caucasian when I was actually a Negro. "I'm not stupid," I replied. "If I checked off 'Negro,' I'd get the worst job over here."

While this exchange was underway, a long line of complaining soldiers was building up behind us. They had a legitimate reason to gripe. It was hot and humid, and the air reeked with the odor of night soil—human excrement the Koreans used for manure. Finally, the warrant officer dropped the argument and gave me instructions regarding my duty assignment. I'm guessing that after I left he corrected my form to read "Negro."

Nevertheless, my first assignment was considered a plum. It was at South Korea's main military post office—the Seoul APO—as a postal clerk. I'm sure that, if he'd had the power, the warrant officer would have assigned me to the Eighth Cavalry or some other front-line unit.

But I wasn't at the Seoul APO very long before being transferred. I suspect that the reason was that I was still complaining about racial discrimination; the differences this time included a letter-writing campaign that I'll discuss a bit later. My new assignment was to Company B EUSA Signal Long Line Battalion, based in Taegu, a city in the southern part of the country. I didn't fit in well and was assigned minor tasks such

as taking and typing the "morning report" and a few other mostly cleri-
cal chores. That left me with considerable time to myself, which I used
to study Tang Soo Do, a Korean form of karate. I trained almost every
evening at an off-post Korean gym under the tutelage of my instructor,
Sun Song Gee. I managed to acquire a first-degree black belt.

My very light duties also afforded time for reading and thinking—
thinking about my future. I was twenty-four years old, and I came to the
conclusion that if I didn't get started pretty soon, I'd never amount to
anything. In the letters and tape recordings Connie and I exchanged,
we discussed our plans when I got discharged. We agreed that we were
going to work our butts off to save money. And as soon as we saved $700,
we would move to Los Angeles, and I would enroll in college.

Meanwhile, my letter-writing campaign against discrimination began
in earnest, including letters to Representative Robert Nix of Philadelphia and the Department of the Army's chief surgeon general and
inspector general. In addition, I started writing letters to newspapers.
A December 1960 issue of The Philadelphia Independent printed my rather
lengthy letter in its entirety—on the front page, no less, under the title
"A GI In Korea Looks At U.S. Bias" The letter, which detailed racial discrimination and shabby military practices, stirred considerable controversy. (See pages 58–59.)

Government authorities must have taken an interest in my newspaper
allegations. Connie said that several of her neighbors told her of visits by
FBI agents making inquiries about her because she was my wife.

I have no idea whether I was the subject of similar investigations while
in Korea, but several high-ranking officers questioned me. One asked
what I was doing with all the letter writing and just what was my problem? Prefacing my response with "In all due respect, sir," I told him that
I'd taken an oath to defend my country against enemies both foreign and
domestic and that I see those who support or tolerate racial discrimination as a domestic enemy.

My assertions, of course, angered the officers. They argued that I was
mistaken about the level of racial discrimination in the Army and that
great progress had been made, including the integration of all military forces. I countered by pointing to the fact that, as a black person, I

With my karate instructors as a GI in Taegu, South Korea.

LOCAL AND NATIONAL EDITION

THE PHILADELPHIA INDEPENDENT

THE WORLD'S GREATEST NEGRO TABLOID

RED. U.S. PATENT OFFICE   1P

THE VOICE OF THE PEOPLE

ol. 30 — No. 51   Philadelphia, Pa.   SATURDAY, DECEMBER 17, 1960   12c Philadelphia — Elsewhere 15c

A GI In Korea Looks At U. S. Bias

"I, as a soldier, at one time, could not summon one reason why I should serve in the Armed Forces. But after much thought, I came up with one reason: and that is, to preserve the freedom that we have already gained, and to have the right to fight. This freedom that Negroes have already gained has been hard fought and each right has cost dearly. This is what I claim to be protecting . . ."

The foregoing statement was contained in a letter to the INDEPENDENT from an American GI. The soldier, whom we shall call "Joe," has written without rancor or bitterness. And in so doing, he invites careful thought and consideration to what he has to say. In publishing "Joe's" letter, we are proud to say that he has the courage of his convictions and did not ask that his name be withheld.

Dear Editor:

Enclosed herewith is a brief outline of my military career and some of the race problems that I have encountered. This information is factual to the best of my knowledge and I am forwarding this news to you because I believe that the public should become cognizant of the injustices inflicted upon the Negro soldier in the United States Army. I wasn't aware of many of these things before I was drafted into the Army and I believe that through publication of this article, I may spare other young men the shock that I encountered.

Your office has my expressed consent to print this material and to alter or delete it as you see fit. I expect no consideration other than the intrinsic value that I will derive if you see fit to publish this article. Please advise me how I might be able to contribute to the betterment of the Negro race.

* * *

IN THE PAST DECADE, there has been a steady decline of world prestige once held by the United States. A country does not lose prestige for no reason. A major reason why we have lost prestige could be the lack of coherence between what we preach and with is actually practiced in our country.

For instance, we pay "lip service" to such rules of government as those which protect the individual's rights, but when it comes to actual practice, we are silent. There are many places in the United States where, because of color, citizens are denied the right to vote, the right to attend public schools of their own choosing, and many other individual benefits of a democratic society.

This problem is not only the concern of the Negro seeking status equality, but of all persons sincerely interested in the welfare of the United States. This social problem could lead to more magnitudinous proportions than we could ever dream.

Right now we are imbued with the task of trying to win Africa to the side of the West, or at least strengthen the relationship. Can we go into Africa preaching democracy and peace in view of the racial strife that exists in our country? Can we honestly send our diplomats out to tell the darker peoples of the world that the United States is their friend?

We, ourselves, are supplying the Communists with a weapon propaganda to use against us in our relations with Africa. And if we don't change U.S. policies toward the Negro within our country, all the colored peoples of the world will lose faith in us and turn to a system which appears to offer more hope.

That action would mean the loss of manpower, raw materials, and a market without which the West could not survive. More than that, such action might even mean the destruction of the free world. The move would completely upset the precarious balance of power which now exists.

Some may say that whites are discriminated against, too, because of race, religion, place of birth, or poverty. But that type of discrimination doesn't have the quality that crushes the spirit and robs the individual of ambition and hope.

I refer to signs reading "No Colored", or homes bombed because a family chose to exercise the right to vote. I refer to a Negro being beaten half to death because he chooses not to be submissive, or a solder—far away from home—reading in a newspaper of Negroes being denied justice even while he, the soldier, is defending democracy.

Truly it can be said that the Negro does not enjoy his share of the benefits of democracy. The Negro today, in this age of enlightenment, is still expected to play the role of the submissive, docile slave. He was often lynched for being spirited and demanding his rights; and to justify this brutality, the white man usually constructed elaborate rationalizations such as "rape" or to "uphold the dignity of the white woman."

Today, the white man's rationalizations to justify depriving the Negro of his rights are much more subtle. Recently, in the Army Times magazine, it was disclosed that a personnel unit in Korea was identifying Negro troops by marking X's on the back of a particular card used in administration. Also it disclosed the fact that there are amazingly few Negro Sergeant Majors in the Army.

The Army has gone far since the time of the all-out segregated Army, but the job of completely integrating the Armed Forces is far from completion.

The Army has played a major part toward the improvement of race relations in the United States. Some men, for the first time in their lives, learn that the Negro is not the stereotyped individual of the cartoons. They learn that people do not have a repulsive odor because of color. They learn that the Negro is intelligent and not just capable of manual labor, but of highly professional and skilled jobs.

Moreover, they learn that the Negro, if given equal opportunity, is their equal as a fighter, an administrator, and, above all, a human being.

I entered the Army and was sent South for the first time in my life. I was shocked by signs reading "White" and "Colored" but I thought surely there would be equality on government posts.

After basic training, I was sent to Fort Stewart, Georgia. I saw segregated dances at this post. I wrote to the Department of the Army and this situation was changed to no dances at all. At that post, many Negroes were given menial tasks such as sanitation details and grass cutting. There were no Negroes as section leaders in my company.

While at Fort Stewart, because of my protests, my Commanding Officer and my section leader conspired against me and I was court-martialed. Thereupon, I proved to the court beyond reasonable doubt that both were conspiring against me and, consequently, I was found not guilty.

Shortly after this incident, I was shipped to Korea before I could obtain redress against the officer for undue hardship upon a person subject to his command.

The Army should not be allowed to send a man to an area of the United States where he will be subject to mistreatment because of race.

Negro men have lain dead on the battlefield. One has to think for a while when asked, "What did he die for?" Negroes have fought in six major wars for the United States. One might ask what more does a man have to do to prove that he is worthy of consideration as a first class citizen.

Foreigners come to our country and—as they pass through the immigration

Source: Walter Williams, letter to the editor, *The Philadelphia Independent,* December 17, 1960.

station—they have already more consideration and reap more benefits of democracy than the Negro native who has been in the United States for over three centuries.

Being stationed in Korea has helped me immeasurably to make a clearer observation of the "race problem" in the United States. I have been invited (but did not accept the invitation) on several occasions to accompany white soldiers on their "outings" to sexually exploit the Korean women.

As my reader can see, this hospitality is taboo in the United States. Therefore, one can see just where the problems of the races lie; it is the fear of miscegenation in the minds of the Southern bigots. Or more accurately, I should say, it is the fear of the pro-segregationists, wherever they are.

Especially those who are so foolish as to think that children of elementary grade set off to school with matrimonial ideas in their minds. Or they fear that by mingling, children would find that the "facts" their parents taught them about Negroes are altogether false, and, consequently, the "color line" would be crushed and a warm relationship brought about that might lead to interracial marriage.

My reader should not construe that this idea of interracial marriage is the goal of desegregation of schools and other public facilities; for the ultimate goal of desegregation is to bring equality to people of all races.

In Korea, I have noticed what might be called discrimination in the Armed Forces. But the practices in force over here are difficult to prove as discrimination in a court of law.

(To be concluded next week)

EDITOR'S NOTE. The conclusion of a two-part article telling the true experiences of an American GI who has faced American-made discrimination and segregation both in America and in Korea where he is now stationed. We believe this soldier typifies the real American Negro who has not defected to Communism despite the walls of prejudice which surround him on all sides. More than that, we are confident that it will be young men like this soldier who will be tomorrow's leaders of the American black man; men who will not sell their birthright for a mess of pottage in the form of personal gain or glory, but who will place their stakes for equality before the law for the Negro everywhere, and will not be content until the goal is won.

•

A GI's story is concluded from last week:

In Korea, I have noticed what might be called discrimination in the Armed Forces. But the practices in force over here are difficult to prove as discrimination in a court of law.

In existence are such things as Negroes not holding key jobs such as in the United Nations Command Headquarters or other key administrative jobs.

If one were to investigate this allegation, he would find a few Negroes acting more or less as figure-heads in positions just for the purpose of keeping down dissatisfaction, or to refute statements that might be made of discrimination in the Army.

Before getting my present assignment, I was assigned to an Army unit in Seoul; I was able to witness the overwhelming proportion of white soldiers as compared to the Negro soldiers there.

Mostly Combat

Most Negroes, regardless of their qualifications, who are assigned to the Far East Command are assigned combat type duties; which is to say, one would find very few Negroes assigned to administrative type positions.

The personnel section might argue this statement by saying that there aren't qualified Negroes to hold "front office" type positions. Even if this were the case, the reason could be traced back to segregation in that Negroes were not, in any sizable amount, being trained to hold key jobs.

And if one were to say that Negroes were not even qualified to be trained to hold such jobs, that, too, could be traced back to segregation and discrimination in that they did not receive the proper basic education.

The whole world is cognizant of the "race problem" in the United States and we as Americans are on stage.

'White Supremacy'

In Korea, a country highly subjected to Communist influence, it is of utmost importance that we show these people what United States democracy is. But—are we doing that? My answer is "No."

An observing individual has only to be in Korea a short time to see that "white supremacy" is being taught to the Koreans. This policy, I'm happy to say, is not of the higher commanders, but of a minority of white soldiers.

These bigoted soldiers have told the Koreans that Negroes are "houseboys" in the United States. Moreover, these soldiers have taught the Koreans to call Negroes "niggers," and have told them not to wash their clothes with the "colored man's."

These things I have experienced. For instance, one day while walking on the main supply route, I passed some Korean teenagers; as I passed, they broke out singing "Old Black Joe" in a harassing manner.

The Other Side

However, I am glad that this is not the attitude of the learned and respectable Korean people. The Koreans who choose to assume the "white supremacy" attitude are in the minority and, by and large, comprise the prostitutes who earn a better living by adhering to this type attitude.

I have talked to many intelligent Koreans who are very much aware of the "race problem" in the United States and can see the superiority attitude reflected against them, too. Some have told me that the Korean people like the Negro GI better because he doesn't assume the superior attitude in his relationship with them, or look down upon them as if they were dirt.

And this is not to say that the Negro GI is totally free of guilt insofar as a superior attitude is concerned. There are a few who are as overbearing in their manner as the most bigoted of the white soldiers.

The rub is that the Negro who does this lacks the intelligence to realize that when he returns to the United States, he will resume the place as a scapegoat.

Refuge for Scoundrels

This problem of race difficulties is truly magnitudinous. I have no practical suggestions to solve it overnight. But I do hold to this thought:

The law bodies cannot legislate love amongst men, but they can legislate equality under law. But not even this has been achieved.

I, as a soldier, at one time, could not summon one reason why I should serve in the Armed Forces. But after much thought, I came up with one reason: and that is, to preserve the freedom that we have already gained and to have the right to fight. This freedom that Negroes have already gained has been hard fought and each right has cost dearly.

This is what I claim to be protecting.

My criticism of United States policies has been looked upon by some authorities as disloyalty, but I say:

To look at only the good and turn one's face from the bad is not loyalty in the broadest meaning of the word. And, too, democracy is not a democracy when one cannot criticize it and change what is wrong to right. It becomes a "refuge for scoundrels posing as patriots."

Soldier's Wife Is Thankful

To the Editor:

I am writing in sincere gratitude and appreciation for your publication of my husband's articles on racial bias in these United States. I am extremely grateful to you, and also very proud of him. I only regret that you couldn't use his name. I should like my husband to be known to everyone who reads the article; but I must admit I would fear for his life.

He has been threatened several times. I don't know whether he mentioned those times to you I'm afraid I have nothing to contribute to his article, as I think he has said everything that could be said. I couldn't have put it as well as he anyway.

I don't wish to be repetitious, but I'd like to thank you again for my husband and myself. We are sincerely grateful, happy, and very proud that you saw fit to publish his articles. Thank you.
Sincerely,

Name Withheld

didn't have the same civilian constitutional guarantees that white soldiers enjoyed, and I wanted to know the nature of my obligations in that light.

Thinking back on some of these confrontations, I wonder why at least one officer wasn't honest and straightforward enough to say, "Look soldier, I understand and agree with your grievances, but I have a mission. Your conduct is sabotaging that mission, and if you continue, I'm going to see to it that you're jailed." Instead, the officers always sought to convince me that things weren't that bad and were actually getting better.

It was my guess then, and still is, that these officers were not racists. Some exchanged pleasantries with me from time to time. One of them arranged an appointment for me to have a discussion with a black army chaplain. He spoke at length about what the Army was a few years back and what great progress had been made since his enlistment. I told him that since blacks didn't enjoy the same liberties at home that whites enjoyed, I didn't think we ought to be on the front lines, risking our lives. At that point, he asked me whether I thought we should turn back the clock to a time when blacks weren't in fighting units but in service units comprised of truck drivers and quartermaster troops. He maintained that the placement of blacks in fighting units was one of the achievements of desegregation.

Toward the end of our meeting, he told me, "Private Williams, you catch more flies with honey than vinegar." I remember thinking to myself, *What an Uncle Tom!* Thinking back, I realize that I was wrong and the chaplain was right.

Going Home

In mid-June 1961, I took a train from Taegu to Seoul and then a bus to Inchon for embarkation to Oakland. My tour in Korea was complete, and I was going to be discharged from active duty. First came another nineteen-day ocean voyage that seemed to have no end. In Oakland, I received my official (and honorable) discharge from active duty, my mustering-out pay, and an airplane ticket to Philadelphia. Connie, my mother, Pops, and my nephew met me at the airport. On the way home,

Pops, ever considerate, whispered in my ear that he had arranged for my mother to fix an early dinner so Connie could show me the apartment she had rented for us. The apartment was actually a bedroom that doubled as a living room, plus a kitchenette; the bathroom had to be shared with a person who lived in the rear. But it was a nice place and in a nice section of Germantown.

I got my job back with Yellow Cab and started working in early July. Since Connie was employed at a costume-jewelry factory, we instituted our plan to save money to move to Los Angeles. In our exchanges of letters, while I was in Korea, Connie agreed with my idea of making that move; she was less than enthusiastic about it when I returned home. She was not as adventurous as I and wondered whether we could make it out West. The farthest she had been from Philadelphia was to visit her brother in Buffalo.

One of the things that helped convince her was my saying that even if we wound up on welfare, welfare was better in Los Angeles than in Philadelphia. Also, I told her that we would set aside enough money to return to Philadelphia if we found we couldn't make it in Los Angeles. Those arguments, in addition to the fact that we were truly in love, allayed most of Connie's fears.

By December, we had saved more than $900, and we took off for Los Angeles in my 1951 Mercury. The car was towing a 4′ × 6′ U-Haul trailer containing all of our worldly possessions. We arrived around six o'clock on a Sunday morning, had coffee and doughnuts in a coffee shop, then began our search for an apartment. We rented a nice one for $65 a month. In January 1962, Connie found a job working at Consumer Credit Corporation (CCC) earning $55 a week. In February, I was admitted to California State College/Los Angeles (later a university), intending to pursue a bachelor's degree in sociology.

In the Active Reserve

The history of my military career would be incomplete without at least a brief recounting of what happened when I served the balance of my military obligation. When I was drafted, one's military obligation came

Moving to Los Angeles in 1961, with Connie and me in my '51 Mercury and all of our worldly possessions in a 4′ × 6′ U-Haul trailer.

in three parts: two years of active duty, two years of active-*reserve* duty, and two years of *inactive*-reserve duty, for a total obligation of six years.

In Los Angeles, therefore, I was assigned to an active-reserve unit in North Hollywood. For a brief time, I was the only black person in the unit. Meetings could not have been more than once a month, and most of the time they involved classes of one kind or another, e.g., map reading, how to shoot an azimuth, survival training. When I attended reserve meetings, I always took my schoolbooks and homework and studied. At one meeting, I had papers laid out on a table, doing my homework, when a lieutenant I hadn't seen before came up and addressed me in a very officious manner:

"Soldier what's your job here?" I responded, "Sir, my job is to integrate this unit, and once I sign in the unit is integrated and my job is done." The officer looked stunned. He said nothing else to me as he turned away and nearly walked into a pole supporting the roof. Nor did anyone else bring up that exchange to me. Someone might have told the officer to leave well enough alone, because if I was working on school assignments, at least I wasn't causing any disruption.

And I did cause disruptions. During one escape-and-evasion training class, an officer was lecturing about his experiences when separated from his unit during the Korean War. I raised my hand to ask a question: "Why should I, as a black man, have to worry about capture?" I explained that both Koreans and I were victims of the white man's oppression, and once the Korean soldier recognized that, we'd both realize that we were friends, not enemies. My argument was ludicrous and disruptive as well, as I intended. As noted earlier, one of the talents that I honed to perfection during my military career was that of being able to say the most ridiculous things with the most sincere and honest face while laughing like crazy inside as I was taken seriously.

While a reservist, I continued my letter-writing campaign against racial injustices—both in the military and in society at large. I wrote a letter to President John Kennedy. The assistant secretary of defense replied with the most reasonable response that I received from any official. (See pages 64–65.) Shortly thereafter, I received a call from someone in the assistant secretary's office telling me of a form I could fill out requesting a hardship release from further active-reserve duty. I followed that suggestion, making up a story about conflict between school and work obligations, and was released from active reserve duty. In 1965, I received an honorable-discharge certificate.

My time in the military was indeed valuable—even though, as my stepfather had suggested when I was drafted, I wouldn't do it again for a million dollars. I matured a lot during those two years of active duty. The most important part of the maturation process was deciding that, if I was ever going to make something of myself, I'd better make a plan and get busy following it. Leaving Philadelphia for Los Angeles was my life's single best decision. Best, that is, save one: my decision to make Connie Taylor my wife and establish a partnership that lasted until her death nearly forty-eight years later.

Walter E. Williams
2225 So Harvard Blvd.
Los Angeles 18, Calif
May 29th 1963

The President
Washington, D.C.

Dear Sir:

Through no choosing of my own, I am presently a member in
Company "C" 3rd Battalion, 30th Infantry, U.S. Army Reserves,
located at 5525 Vineland Avenue, North Hollywood, California. I
find it necessary to consult you as Commander-in-Chief of the Armed
Forces in pursuit of a satisfactory answer to my problem which is:
I, as an American Negro, in view of disfranchisement, in view of
injustice, in view of the humiliation and frustration that I suffer
because my skin is black, in view of the discrimination that break
and crush the spirit of men, and in view of this Administration's
apparent tolerance of these evils— I want to know the nature of
my obligation to Armed Forces of America relative to my Caucasian
counterpart.

In other words, I well understand my obligation as well as
the white soldier's; but, he, in return, receives or better stated
has the potential to receive any and all benefits of democracy while
I get little. Even more irritating is that this white soldier
may have a father who was a Nazi and murdered many Americans in
World War II. But this soldier whose loyalty is yet to be tested
already enjoys more fruits of democracy that I or any other Negro
have yet to appreciate, even though the Negro has proven his loyalty
in at least five major war.

My question to you is: Should Negroes be relieved of their
service obligation or continue defending and dying for empty promises
of freedom and equality......should young Negroes answer the draft
call? Should Negroes continue support through taxes funds that
are not equitably distributed? Or should we, as the great founders
of our country, disobey that which is wrong and that which supports
wrong. Should we perpetuate this injustice by pacifist movements.
Or should we demand human rights as our Founding Fathers did at the
risk of being called extremists. At the risk of any name that might
be applied against me, I contend that we relieve ourselves of
oppression in a manner that is in keeping with the great heritage
of our nation.

In closing I admit that this problem is a difficult and trying
but I cannot in honesty to my country and to my people accept
"second class" citizenship for no American.

Respectfully yours,

Walter E Williams

Source: In the author's possession.

ASSISTANT SECRETARY OF DEFENSE
WASHINGTON 25, D.C.

MANPOWER

18 September 1963

Mr. Walter E. Williams
2225 South Harvard Boulevard
Los Angeles, California

Dear Mr. Williams:

Your letter of 29 May addressed to the President has been
referred to me for reply. I regret the delay in acknowledging it, but I think that in the several months that
have passed since you wrote the President many actions
have been taken which are responsive to the kinds of
questions you raised.

Your principal question was "Should the Negro be relieved
of his military obligation or should he continue defending
and dying for empty promises of freedom and equality..."
A long history of willingness by American Negroes to bear
the burdens and responsibilities of citizenship while
denied many of its privileges furnishes a remarkable
testimonial of Negro commitment to the American ideal.
I believe that with the enactment of pending legislation,
with the implementation of the recent Defense Department
directive requiring military commanders to foster equal
opportunity off-base for members of their commands, and
with countless other on-going efforts by men of good
will, very significant and beneficial changes are being
and will be made in the status of Negroes in America.
While I do not mean to suggest that the millennium will
arrive over night, I am sure there will be considerably
less justification for characterizing the promises of
freedom and equality which are extended to all citizens
as "empty" for some of them.

Very truly yours,

Alfred B. Fitt
Deputy Assistant Secretary
(Civil Rights)

Source: In the author's possession.

CHAPTER FOUR

Heading West for Opportunity

FEBRUARY 1962 FOUND ME ENROLLED as a full-time student at California State College/Los Angeles (majoring in sociology). Although our finances were meager, we managed fairly well, thanks to the savings we accumulated in Philadelphia and a sound budgeting system. Our modest first-floor apartment was a former mansion in a fairly nice neighborhood—2225 South Harvard Boulevard—that had been made into six units. The living room doubled as a bedroom, and space next to the bathroom provided me with a quiet study area. The apartment rented for $65 a month.

We managed our money through a "brown-envelope" system. One envelope, for rent, received a certain amount from each of Connie's paychecks. Other envelopes held what we needed to pay for food and household supplies, clothing, tuition and books, and entertainment. We also had an envelope labeled "extra." That's where we'd put money that was left over from the other envelopes.

Connie didn't share my habits of thrift; she called it being cheap. We had many minor arguments over expenditures. Looking back, some of our arguments bordered on the ridiculous—like the one over peanut butter. Connie wanted the Skippy brand. I wanted the store brand because it was cheaper, but she complained about the taste of that one and the fact that the oil settled on top. I offered to stir the contents so that they were smooth, like Skippy, but to no avail. Skippy prevailed as our peanut butter. Nevertheless, indeed, in later years, I overheard Connie recommending our envelope system to members of her family.

Food shopping was quite an adventure. It often took us to five or six different stores. From advertisements in the neighborhood paper, we'd find out which stores had items on sale, so-called loss leaders, that we wanted to buy. One establishment might offer five forty-six-ounce cans of pineapple juice for a dollar. Another might have eight cans of tuna fish for a dollar—resulting in many a tuna-casserole dinner. We'd purchase the items on sale and then drive to the next store. On Saturdays, we'd drive downtown to the Grand Central Market at 3rd Street and South Broadway to buy meat and fresh vegetables. We took advantage of street parking on Hill Street and walked down very steep steps to the market. Loaded down with bags of groceries we'd spend a nickel each to ride the Angels Flight cable car back up to Hill Street.

Another shopping strategy involved the several Los Angeles supermarkets that were open 24 hours a day. That was an unheard-of novelty to us at the time; there was no such practice in Philadelphia. Some of these markets would have overnight sales. So while Connie slept, I'd shop—at three or four o'clock in the morning.

We also saved money by purchasing what were called "checks and dirty" eggs—unwashed, with external imperfections—from Don Ray's supermarket, around the corner from our apartment. We effected other savings through such tricks as mixing whole milk with powdered milk.

Connie, unlike I, was an instant friend to most people. She had a wonderful, outgoing personality and was very trusting of people and lots of fun to be around. We received regular invitations from her friends to play cards, join a party, or go out somewhere. I frequently got the impression that the only reason I was at the event was that they couldn't have Connie without me.

Thanks to her, I am, in important ways, not quite the person today that I was back then. I recall occasions when we'd return home after a party or some other social event and Connie would deliver what amounted to a lecture on good manners: "Did you really have to say that to So and So? Do you have to prove to people that you're smarter than they are?" In

My mother and
Connie, circa 1962.

short, she became a civilizing and humanizing influence in my life, and
I'm indebted to her for it.

Years later, a discussion of the different ways Connie and I viewed
the world would become an important eye-opener for me. When I was
a graduate student at UCLA, Professor Armen Alchian and I were having one of our needling-type discussions during a faculty-student coffee
hour. I told the professor that I preferred making a "Type I" error with
respect to acquaintances, while my wife would rather make a "Type II"
error. I meant, I said, that I assumed people were my enemies until they
proved themselves my friends. Connie assumed people she'd just met
were friendly until they proved themselves otherwise.

I explained further that my vision minimized the chances that I'd be
betrayed at a cost of minimizing the number of friends I'd have. Connie's

vision would yield the reverse. I was impressed by my own exposition to Professor Alchian, until, that is he completely took the wind out of my sails. He said with a grin, "Williams, there's a third alternative that I'd urge you to consider."

"What is that?" I asked.

"Have you considered that people don't give a damn about you one way or another?"

Perhaps our discussion was interrupted; but in any case Professor Alchian, as he frequently did, elaborated no further. He simply planted a seed for thought and left it to grow—or not. Across the intervening decades, right down to today, I've concluded that Alchian was probably right.

By today's standards, Connie and I had a lot of fun on the cheap. During our first year or so in Los Angeles, we often enjoyed packing a picnic lunch, filling the car with gas, doing some sightseeing, then finding a park or a roadside rest area in which to eat before returning home. We'd drive to what were then inexpensive places, like Knott's Berry Farm, or to the Mojave Desert; or we'd tour the Hollywood area and marvel at the homes of movie stars. On Connie's paydays, we'd often treat ourselves to dinner out by buying ten tacos for a dollar, eating them in the car, then going to a neighborhood or drive-in movie.

Once, when we had accumulated eighty dollars in our "extra" envelope, we drove to San Francisco. That sum more than paid for three days' and two nights' worth of expenses. We rented a fairly nice hotel room for eight dollars. Our first evening's dinner was at Tarantino's at Fisherman's Wharf. I think that cost us about fifteen dollars, which meant no more restaurant dinners during the trip. Instead, we made do with cheap breakfasts and, later in the day, what was called a walk-away crab salad. We would also buy loaves of San Francisco's famous sourdough bread. The butter we bought to go with it we'd put on the hotel windowsill overnight to stay cool.

We spent our days sightseeing: a boat ride around Alcatraz, visits to Coit Tower and the Golden Gate Bridge. Amazingly, we returned to Los Angeles with eight dollars left over. It was the best vacation that either one of us ever had.

In Jail Again

My last brush with the law occurred late one night after Connie and I had an argument. I have no recollection of what we argued about, but I got dressed and left the apartment in an attempt to walk off my anger. It was a very long walk from our place to the downtown business district. When I left downtown, headed toward home, a policeman in his patrol car pulled up and asked me what I was doing in the area. He had every right to be suspicious. It must have been one or two o'clock in the morning. I replied that I was taking a walk.

"Where do you live?" he asked. I told him, and he said, "That's a long way. You walked all this distance?"

"Yes," I retorted, "and it might be a good idea if you guys got out of your cars and walked around yourselves."

That wisecrack provoked him, and he asked me for identification. I gave him my driver's license, and he phoned in the information. Standing beside the car, I heard the voice of a police radio dispatcher saying that although there were no searches for me, there was an arrest warrant for failing to appear in court for traffic violations. And indeed there was: in Los Angeles, in 1957, I had received several tickets for illegal parking, but because I was about to leave the city, I decided to ignore them. So now, in the wee hours, I was arrested and taken to jail.

That was bad enough. Worse, I had to call Connie, after our argument, to come downtown to post bond for me. She didn't have enough money, so she called my father, and they both came to the police station, and I was released and given a court date. When I appeared in court a few days later, I lied to the judge, telling him that I hadn't paid the 1957 tickets because I'd been drafted into the Army and hadn't received the notices. The judge dismissed the late-payment penalties, allowing me to pay only the original parking fine, which couldn't have been more than $50.

Not Becoming an Economist—Almost

I found myself enjoying life as a full-time student, and academically I was doing very well. During my junior year at Cal State, I came to the conclusion that sociology wasn't for me, and changed my major to economics. That decision was heavily influenced by my summer reading of W.E.B. DuBois's *Black Reconstruction*. My first economics class, in principles of microeconomics, resulted in a near-disaster: I received a grade of D.

Professor Cole, the instructor, and I didn't get along very well. Whatever my classroom questions and comments were, they irritated him. After the mid-term examination, when I received a low grade, he called me to his office. I should, he said, switch from economics to a different major. Getting a D was emotionally devastating, and I was going to take the professor's advice. But Connie, supportive as always, persuaded me to take another economics class and see what would happen. I therefore enrolled in Professor Arthur Kirsch's intermediate microeconomics class.

This time, I earned an A on all of his examinations, scoring the highest or next-to-highest grade in the class. Professor Kirsch frequently called on me with a question and complimented me on my answers. Students also questioned me prior to exams. You can't imagine what that did for my ego. I was the only black student in the class, and I relished having all those white students looking up to me!

My performance in Kirsch's class was truly confidence-building, and it tended to confirm Connie's blunt assessment of Professor Cole—that he was a racist s.o.b. I'm not sure whether he was a racist, but he was definitely an s.o.b.

Except for Professor Jean Tipton's intermediate macroeconomics class, in which I received only a C, I did well in other courses in the field. Professor Kirsch became my friend as well as my teacher and advisor. He invited me to his house to talk, and he gave me books to read. He and his wife, Peggy, invited Connie and me to their house every year to have Christmas dinner with their friends and relatives. On several occasions, they even treated us to dinner at the Nine Muses, a very nice restaurant that we ourselves could not have afforded.

From a Near-Disaster to Easy Street

Everything was going quite well until Connie became ill in the spring of 1963. Suffering a miscarriage, she was hospitalized and unable to work for several months. For survival, we depended on our savings, the $700 or so that we brought to Los Angeles and deposited in the bank. Things weren't looking good. We got down to $35 in our account at Security National Bank.

Fortunately, I landed a summer job with my father doing construction work. Due mostly to Connie's aggressive intervention, he and I had gotten over our differences. My father was a well-respected lather in and secretary of Los Angeles Local 42 of the Wood, Wire and Metal Lathers union. He taught me how to hang the Sheetrock that served as a foundation for plaster walls and ceilings of houses. My pay was very good, and Connie and I managed well through the summer. But what was I going to do in the fall? With Connie convalescing, I faced the prospect of dropping out of college to find a job to support us.

No less than a miracle happened. Earlier in the year, I had applied for a job with the Los Angeles County Probation Department, and in September, I was called in for an interview. I was prepared for another disappointment because I'd just endured one with regard to a different job. Carey Jenkins, a classmate who was a part-time employee at a Bank of America branch, had referred me to his supervisor. In filling out the job application, I had to acknowledge my Philadelphia criminal conviction. During the job interview, the manager told me that the conviction disqualified me from employment at the bank. I was devastated and left wondering whether I'd ever be able to get a decent job.

My interview with the county probation department went very well. When the issue of my arrest record arose, I was very comforted by the interviewer; he and his colleagues, he said, were far more influenced by my more-recent past and my prospects for the future. I was hired as a probation attendant. My earnings would be $5,200 a year plus a mileage allowance. Connie and I were off the financial hook.

Landing that position was a godsend in several ways. A probation attendant's job was to oversee a county juvenile detention camp while the resident counselors slept. I called it big-time babysitting. There were ten such facilities scattered through remote forest areas of Los Angeles County, and I was assigned to one of them, Camp Mendenhall, near Palmdale. Although Mendenhall was sixty-five miles from our house, I didn't mind the trip too much. I liked driving, I received a generous mileage allowance, and in the 1960s, Los Angeles traffic was not the nightmare it has become.

I was one of the probation department's several "relief men." That is, I didn't have a permanent camp assignment, but filled in for probation attendants who were on vacation, sick, or absent for some other reason. I worked from 10:00 P.M. until 6:00 A.M., when a resident counselor who was a probation officer relieved me.

Working at night meant that I could continue my studies as a full-time student. In addition, it meant that I had a lot of time to study. Most days, when I reported to work, the camp's 90 to 100 boys were already bedded down for the night; if a few were still awake, they'd soon be asleep. So after spending an hour or so completing camp paperwork, I had the rest of my shift to myself. Generally, the only interruption would be a boy requesting permission to go to the bathroom, although there was an occasional disturbance that required my attention.

Another bonus was that I could eat all I wanted. Very often, the camp's cook would prepare and deliver a late dinner for the "night man." When a cook was off duty, I'd stop by the kitchen, fix my own meal for the night, and carry it to the dormitory's control center.

Finishing at six in the morning meant that I could get to school in time for an eight o'clock class. I took classes back to back so that I could leave campus by early afternoon to go home and sleep. The probation department gave me a work schedule that pleased not only me but my colleagues as well—because I chose to work weekends most of the time. Having my two days off during the week eased my college schedule.

Connie eventually recovered from her illness and then landed a job as a clerk at the Federal Reserve Bank. With two paychecks coming in, we were able to enjoy a middle-class life. We moved to a much nicer apartment—actually, a charming little house behind the landlady's larger house, on Cloverdale Avenue in West Los Angeles. I purchased my first brand-new car—a 1963 Volvo—as well as a used car for Connie. We took trips to Mexico and drove across the country to visit our families, who were proud of the success that we made of ourselves. We were able to do things for them, such as bring Connie's father out to vacation with us.

We were also able to have Connie's older brother, Phil, who was imprisoned for armed robbery, paroled to our custody. Since I worked for the Los Angeles County Probation Department, it was an easy matter getting the Graterford prison authorities to agree to that. Phil had been convicted of driving the getaway car for an armed robbery. He lived with us for several months while he looked for a job and his own apartment.

From Cal State to UCLA

In the summer of 1965, I graduated from California State College with a bachelor of arts degree in economics. I hadn't given much thought to graduate school, but Professor Kirsch encouraged me to consider it. And my father's fourth of what would ultimately be five wives told me that Alpha Kappa Alpha, her sorority, and Seagram's Gin were cosponsoring an essay contest and encouraged me to enter in hopes of winning a scholarship. I entered and gave an oral presentation before judges assembled at UCLA. I didn't win; my essay was judged fourth best.

Disappointed, I left the room after the winner was announced. As I was walking down the hall, Harold Summers, one of the judges as well as a dean and faculty member in UCLA's economics department, hailed me. He said that although I hadn't won the scholarship, I should apply for admission to UCLA's graduate school. He pointed out that as far as tuition was concerned, I wouldn't need a scholarship: UCLA's highly subsidized tuition was only $75 a semester. I was soon admitted to the department's masters program, determined to pursue that degree while continuing to work for the county probation department.

A week or so before classes started, I met with the department's graduate advisor, Professor Jack Hirschleifer. He asked me whether I had any questions. I told him that I felt a bit apprehensive about starting graduate school. He looked at my transcript again and told me that I should feel that way. Although my grade-point average was 3.0, most of the department's graduate students had much higher averages. At the time, UCLA's economics department ranked among the top dozen in the country. I was in over my head, and Professor Hirschleifer's assessment turned out to be correct.

During my first semester, I took a grad-level microeconomics theory course taught by Professor Alice Vandermuelan. Virtually all of the material was new to me, but it didn't appear to be that new to most other students in her class. I met with Professor Vandermuelan several times to discuss problems I was having with the course; she was very sympathetic, pointing me to self-help materials. I had a particular problem with the mathematics used in the course: matrix algebra, calculus, and linear programming. She recommended that I read William Baumol's *Economic Theory and Operations Analysis*. That advice was providential; it helped me make it through the class. Other courses I took went fairly well.

In December 1967, I earned a master of arts degree in economics. I had already begun seeking full-time employment teaching the subject. I applied and/or interviewed at a number of California's two-year schools, including Compton, Laney, Glendale, Antelope Valley, and Imperial Valley Colleges, and Santa Monica and Long Beach City Colleges; also Shoreline University in Seattle. In addition, I sent applications to a few four-year colleges and universities: Howard, Morgan State, and Central Michigan.

I received rejection letters from all of those institutions: either they weren't hiring, or another candidate had been selected. I was of course quite disappointed. But I still had my job with the probation department, and a job as a full-fledged probation officer had opened up.

During the summer of 1967, Los Angeles City College notified me that it had available a part-time position to teach an evening course in introductory economics. I jumped at the opportunity: lack of teaching experience was one reason stated for some of the turn-downs I had received in my job-search interviews. And as it turned out, the job at Los Angeles City College convinced me that I wanted a lifetime of teaching.

Early in 1967, I resigned from the probation department. And another job opportunity in higher education came along: Bob Butler, a fellow student and friend, introduced me to Professor Werner Hirsch, a director of UCLA's Institute of Government & Public Affairs Resources for the Future. I was hired as a research assistant to work with Butler, who was one already. The salary was $709 a month. That income plus my earnings from teaching the city-college evening course sufficed to replace the probation department income; in addition, Connie had a full-time job.

Going for It All

I liked graduate school at UCLA. In the course of my masters degree studies, I had the opportunity to meet students in the PhD program. In conversing and debating with them and other graduate students, I became convinced that I was just as smart or almost as smart as they were. Plus, I was willing to spend whatever time and effort were required to learn. I *had* believed that anybody studying for a doctorate had to be a genius— and since I wasn't one, I would settle for a masters. Now I decided that I was going to go further in graduate school. Since I was already a student, I didn't need to apply formally for admission to the PhD program. I simply continued taking classes.

Deciding to pursue a doctorate meant that I had to become virtually a brand-new graduate student; my studies for the masters didn't mean much in terms of preparation. I hadn't taken the challenging theory courses taught by Professors Jack Hirschleifer, Armen Alchian, and Axel Leijonhufvud. Without them, there was little or no hope of success on the PhD theory examination. UCLA's economics department PhD requirements included passing the theory exam and three "field" exams. Then one took an oral examination, with four department faculty members and one outside professor querying you. If you succeeded there, you went on to write a dissertation.

Thus the doctorate program posed, to put it mildly, an extreme challenge for me. But I had an important quality in my favor: the willingness to make whatever sacrifices of time and effort where necessary to succeed.

My years at UCLA coincided with those of campus turmoil across the country. Students were protesting the Vietnam War and racial injustices.

I never participated in the demonstrations, but I did take part in the many arguments and debates with fellow students over the racial situation. Many of them saw me as a radical, which probably was a good assessment—not liberal but a libertarian-type radical. Some thought I might be a Black Panther because I wore dashikis, a beret, and a tiger's tooth necklace that were given to me by my friend Kenny Washington, a star on UCLA's NCAA-winning 1966 basketball team.

As the only black American in my classes, my presence was conspicuous. The two other black students in the PhD program were from Africa—one from Ghana, the other from Sierra Leone. Professor Alchian, who taught the first graduate microeconomics course, took quite a liking to me, though it was not obvious at the time. Although not particularly well organized, he was a brilliant professor and scholar.

As he was fumbling through his briefcase, searching for his lecture notes at the beginning of the class, Alchian would often say, "Williams, I bet you don't know [such and such]." Most of the time, I didn't, but sometimes I did. One time he asked me why would a generation build projects, such as the Brooklyn Bridge, that benefitted not only them but many other generations as well? What's in it for them to provide benefits for future generations?

I didn't have an answer and told him so. Professor Alchian asked other students and shot down what each of them said. For the next three or four weeks, he'd spend a few minutes at the beginning of class asking whether anyone had come up with the answer and then if a student offered one, show why it was wrong.

Finally, I thought I had the answer. I said that present generations didn't give a hoot about the welfare of future generations. However, to build a bridge sturdy enough to support hundreds of thousands of tons each hour, one could not avoid building in durability as an unintended by-product. I was quite proud of myself. But Alchian shot me down, too, pointing out essentially this: in wartime, the military builds pontoon bridges that can handle thousands of tons of load per hour *without* durability being a by-product. After several weeks of this game, a student asked Professor Alchian to tell us the answer.

He chuckled and said, "I don't know. I wanted to see if any of you knew."

One student in Alchian's class was his daughter, Arlene. We became friends, had coffee together, and studied together. She told me that her father really enjoyed my presence in class. One reason was that, unlike the other students, I didn't see him as the "God of economics." He intimidated most of them.

Alchian was correct about my attitude toward him. Regardless of a person's status, I've never regarded anyone as my better. That attitude might have come from what my stepfather used to say, "Every man stands up to piss, and whatever he is comes after that." In addition, while Professor Alchian knew much more about economics than I did, I could slam-dunk a basketball, and he couldn't. Therefore, I wasn't afraid to say, as I sometimes did in class, "Professor Alchian, I think you're wrong about that."

My fellow students were in awe of someone who'd challenge Professors Alchian and Hirschleifer as I did. One notable challenge occurred when Professor Alchian said to me in class, "Williams, I bet you're against discrimination." I replied that no, I favored discrimination. Smiling, he asked whether that included racial discrimination. "Yes," I said. "I practiced it a lot when I was dating."

Alchian loved to needle people and was trying to trap me but I wouldn't let him do it. He gave up pulling this trick on me, saying with a laugh, "Williams, you're a rascal."

There's one more story about my tête-à-tête confrontations with Professor Alchian. During the Christmas season, he hung a basket of candy outside his office door. One year after the holiday, he posted a message on the faculty/graduate-lounge bulletin board. In placing candy outside his office for several years, the note said, he had observed that the higher-quality pieces were taken before the lower-quality ones, proving two basic economic phenomena: candy is an economic good; and there's a downward-sloping demand curve for candy.

Below the professor's note, I appended my own suggestion that before he reached such a conclusion, he should have checked out the disposition of the candy—because "I've been removing the candy and flushing it down the toilet." Candy, I noted, rots teeth and is therefore an economic bad. I didn't actually flush the stuff; my aim was simply to needle Professor Alchian, who often did that to others.

Although I signed my name to my handiwork, he never commented on it. I'm guessing that he must have gotten a bit of ribbing from his colleagues.

Several months later, the economics department held its annual reception at UCLA's plush Recreation Center, hosting and honoring such distinguished guests as Arthur Burns, chairman of the board of governors of the Federal Reserve Bank. Distinguished members of the university community were invited, as well as graduate students and their wives or girlfriends. At that event, Professor Alchian asked me to introduce him to the charming lady at my side.

"Professor," I replied, "this is my wife, Connie." He stood back in mock surprise: "Williams, I didn't know you were married; you don't act like a married man." He then proceeded to tell Connie about how his daughter Arlene came home late at night and said she'd been "*studying* with Walter." It might be in her best interest, he continued, to visit the department some time to find out what was going on.

After telling Connie it was nice finally to meet her, Alchian walked off, leaving her looking vexed and me speechless. I had indeed studied with Arlene, but nothing was going on romantically. Although Connie ultimately agreed that Alchian was simply needling me, the whole thing required explaining on my part. I'm sure it was Alchian's way of getting even for my note commenting on his candy thesis.

The PhD program was challenging but also a lot of fun—the fun of learning and of meeting so many people, some of whom remain friends today. But a shock laid in store me. In the fall of 1968, sixteen students took the written "theory" examination, and fourteen—including me—flunked. Several of us had studied together, using past exams as our guide. That didn't help: as it happened, the department that very year had hired five or six new faculty members, and it was they who submitted most of the examination questions—all of them unfamiliar to us. Nonetheless, even if a student is unfamiliar with a particular economic question, he should be able to figure out how to answer it.

In the examination's post-mortem, flunking students were assigned to meet with a couple of professors to discuss their performances en route to a decision on whether they would be allowed to remain in the program. I met with Professor Leijonhufvud, who told me that my exam paper was among the worst. Nevertheless, he and his colleagues thought that I had it in me to do better. So I was assigned various journal articles to read and discuss with a faculty member. I did so in meetings with Hirschleifer, Alchian, or Leijonhufvud, responding to their questions about an assigned article.

I recall talking with Professor Leijonhufvud about Mordecai Ezekiel's 1938 article, in *The Quarterly Journal of Economics*, "The Cobweb Theorem." As we discussed it, he would tell me, frustratingly, that what I'd said earlier was inconsistent with what I was saying now: "Go back and read it again, and come back next week."

At one very low point in this process, Professor Leijonhufvud invited Connie and me to his house in the San Fernando Valley for some Swedish "soul food." We had a delightful evening that showed little evidence of his having dressed me down earlier that day. He then helped me by introducing me to the works of economist Kenneth Boulding, particularly *Reconstruction of Economics* and *Image: Knowledge in Life and Society*. Both books lifted my spirits and excited my overall interest in economics.

Axel Leijonhufvud was to become a very important person in my life. Even when we became friends, he maintained an uncanny ability to separate our friendship and mentorship, when, for example, I came before him in his capacity as a member of my dissertation committee.

The sum of all that: when I took the PhD theory examination the following semester, I passed. I subsequently took three "field" examinations (Public Finance, Economic Development, and Economic History of Europe and the United States), earning passing grades in all three on the first try. During the same semester, I passed the PhD oral exam as well.

Flunking economic theory the first time around, I later realized, did have a benefit. It convinced me that UCLA professors didn't care anything about my race: they'd flunk me just as they'd flunk anyone else who didn't make the grade. Their treatment reassured me in terms of my credentials: "Although I'm certainly not UCLA's brightest student," I thought, "I'm at least average." The university's economics professors weren't practicing affirmative action with me.

My professors were decent in another important way. Yes, I had academic deficiencies, as revealed by my performance on the theory examination. It surely would have been easier and cheaper for the department to paper over those deficiencies by making a "racial allowance" for me. Instead, they took their valuable time to coach me. If I received any special treatment because of my race, it might have been in the form of the professors' willingness to help me. I'd knock on Professor Alchian's office door and he'd invite me in. In the case of other students, he'd often tell them that he was busy and couldn't spare the time. Sometimes he didn't even open the door. He'd holler, "Go away! I'm busy."

Another professor who gave me large amounts of his personal time was Larry Kimball, who taught econometrics. He spent evening after evening assisting me with a class project requiring statistical analysis. Computers were just coming into widespread use. Data had to be entered on IBM punch cards and then taken to the computer center. An incorrect keypunch stroke could result in rejection of one's entire project by the computer's statistical program. You could tell you made an error by seeing a single computer-printout sheet waiting in your box. A fat set of printout sheets was a cause for joy, because it meant that at least your program had run.

Successful completion of the PhD examinations satisfied an arrangement I had with Professor John Norby, the economics department chairman at Cal State. The faculty had voted to offer me a full-time, tenure-track assistant professorship if I successfully completed my PhD written and oral exams. When I satisfied that requirement, I quit teaching my single course at Los Angeles City College, accepted the offer from Cal State, and began teaching three courses there in the fall of 1969. I still had a dissertation to produce. But I was able to delay starting it in earnest for nearly a year, while I adjusted to being a full-time professor of economics.

I suspect that I was hired at Cal State as a result of the impressions and friendships I had made there as a student, plus my continued good relationship with Professor Kirsch. The turbulent '60s might have also figured in—a desire or perceived need by the department to have a black faculty member. The economics faculty couldn't have been described as liberal. Philosophically, it was about where I was at the time: conservative/libertarian with a twinge of liberalness on racial matters.

Sometimes I sarcastically, perhaps cynically, say that I'm glad that I received virtually all of my education before it became fashionable for white people to like black people. By that I mean that I encountered back then a more honest assessment of my strengths and weaknesses. Professors didn't hesitate to criticize me—sometimes even to the point of saying, "That's nonsense, Williams."

Like most young people, my philosophical leanings were toward the liberal side of the political spectrum. In the 1964 presidential elections, I voted for Lyndon Johnson over the conservative Barry Goldwater. I thought that higher minimum wages were the way to help poor people, particularly poor black people. That political attitude endured until I had a conversation with a UCLA professor (it might have been Armen Alchian) who asked me whether I most cared about the intentions behind a higher minimum wage or its effects. If I was concerned about the effects, he said, I should read studies by Chicago University Professor Yale Brozen and others about the devastating effects of the minimum wage on employment opportunities for minimally skilled workers.

I probably became a libertarian through exposure to tough-minded professors who encouraged me to think with my brain instead of my heart. Another important exposure was to the works of great philosopher/economists such as Frederick Bastiat, Ludwig von Mises, Friedrich A. Hayek, and Milton Friedman.

As a professor, I have never used my class for proselytizing students, as so many professors do. I think that's academic dishonesty. Personally,

I want students to share my conviction that personal liberty, along with free markets, is morally superior to other forms of human organization. The most effective means of getting them to share it is to give them the tools to be rigorous, tough-minded thinkers.

Initially, my teaching load at Cal State consisted of three introductory economics courses—two microeconomics and one macroeconomics. A year later, I developed a course on the economics of poverty. Because I had a dissertation to complete, department Chairman Norby spared me committee assignments. I enjoyed being a full-time professor. One of the most significant benefits of teaching is that it forces you to learn your subject. For one thing, ego is involved: you don't want to be unprepared in front of a class of students. Another element for me, one of the school's very few black professors, was that I didn't want to confirm any racial stereotype of mental incompetence.

Being a black professor led to calls to become involved with the campus concerns of black students. They invited me to attend meetings of the Black Student Union. I tried to provide guidance with regard to some of the BSU's demands, such as black studies programs and an increase in the number of black faculty. As I was to do later at Temple University, I offered tutorial services for students having trouble in math. One of my efforts, which fell mostly on deaf ears, was an attempt to persuade black students that the most appropriate use of their time as students was to learn their subject as opposed to pursuing a political agenda.

Connie and I liked becoming part of the Cal State faculty community. We were invited to dinners and cocktail parties at the homes of colleagues, and to other faculty functions. Because we were the only black couple present, and because of the turbulent times, we were always the center of attraction, and race was often the topic of conversation.

Connie landed a new job at Steve Sachs's Hollywood poster shop. She loved both the people she met there and the work itself. It led to invitations to parties that included Hollywood celebrities such as Burl Ives, Brock Peters, and artist Peter Max. Celebrities and entertainers had been an important part of Connie's life before she met me. In

Philadelphia, she used to sing and be on stage with the likes of Little Richard and Nancy Wilson. In Los Angeles, in fact, she was offered a singing gig with a popular female vocal group named the Blossoms. She declined, because I protested; I didn't want to risk losing my wife to the nightclub life.

During my time at Cal State, we managed to live mostly on Connie's paycheck, while banking mine. That practice put us in great financial shape down the road—when we purchased and furnished our first home in Chevy Chase, Maryland.

CHAPTER FIVE

Heading East for Opportunity

IN 1970, PROFESSOR GEORGE BORTS of Brown University invited me to join a panel discussing two papers that would be delivered at the American Economic Association's January 1971 meetings in Detroit. The subject was urban economics. My contribution was very well received, and although just three pages went to print, they became my first professional publication.

Professor James Buchanan, whose courses I had taken at UCLA and who also composed and graded my PhD written examination in public finance, recommended me to Dr. Harold Hochman for a research position in his public finance group at the Urban Institute in Washington, D.C. While in Detroit, I had a job interview with Drs. Hochman and Harvey Galper, as well as with others in the public finance group, and they attended the panel session to observe my performance. Before returning home, I received a very attractive offer—$21,000 a year plus fringe benefits—that would be formalized on a later trip to the Urban Institute. A major attraction for me was that I would be able to spend half my time finishing my dissertation, which I had now titled "The Low-Income Market Place."

I accepted the offer and resigned my position at California State College/Los Angeles. The Urban Institute gave Connie and me two fully paid house-hunting trips to Washington. We settled on a very nice house in Chevy Chase, Maryland, a plush suburb just across the line from Washington. In June, movers loaded our household effects plus Connie's

Connie and I in our first house, with my stepfather—Chevy Chase, Maryland.

little Austin automobile. She and I and our cat drove cross-country to our Maryland house, and I started my new job.

Working at the Urban Institute and being in Washington were eye-openers. Professor Alchian anticipated as much: when he learned that I had accepted employment at the Urban Institute, he told me that I was somewhat naïve and that it would do me good to be in Washington to learn how decisions are really made.

Although I mostly worked on my dissertation, I also commented on research done by my close colleagues and other research groups at the institute. If I'm not being paranoid, some people gave me their research to comment upon just to find out what a black "conservative" economist might think.

Most of the researchers in Hal Hochman's public finance group were middle of the road politically, though a couple were "bleeding-heart" liberals. Not long after arriving at the Urban Institute, I was invited to review and comment on a research project involving day care. I don't recall just what made the project and its arguments silly. In private conversation with a couple of the authors, I asked my favorite questions of people who argue that we need this or that government program: what did Americans do before the proposed government program, and why is it needed now? In the case at hand, how was the nation able to survive and prosper from 1787 to 1972 without a government-run or -subsidized day-care program?

I simply returned the project to its authors with a note saying that the document I'd attached fully expressed my ideas about their concerns with regard to orphans and day care. The attachment was a xeroxed copy of Jonathan Swift's "A Modest Proposal," in which he suggests coping with Ireland's twin hunger and orphan problems by taking orphans, fattening them up, and eating them. Swift's most disturbing passage:

> "I have been assured by a very knowing American of my acquaintance in London, that a young healthy child well nursed is at a year old a most delicious, nourishing, and wholesome food, whether stewed, roasted, baked, or boiled. . . ."

I'm sure my mischievous attachment caused considerable angst and comment among the liberals. Because they *were* liberals, confronting a black person to express their hostility about his ideas was probably unthinkable. Several months later, "Bill" Gorham, the institute president, confided to me that some of my co-workers didn't like me.

Another event that affected my popularity involved a Public Broadcasting System call-in show. I was the interviewee, and I believe the topic was educational vouchers. In a friendly chat prior to the interview, the host discovered that Connie and I resided in Chevy Chase, home at that time to very few other blacks. In the course of our on-air discussion, the host casually mentioned where I lived. Callers were already challenging my position on educational vouchers, which would introduce competition as a means to improve black education. Then a caller asked, "Why do you live in Chevy Chase with all those whites instead of with your own people?" Another caller alluded to my having sold out my people.

I considered that question and comment stupid, and as I sometimes do when confronted in that manner, I made light of them. I told the questioner that I was getting old and my back was bothering me, and for that reason, I wanted to live in a neighborhood where I could simply park my car in front of my house without having to carry the engine and battery in every night. That response brought angry rejoinders from a couple of callers, and I learned later that some viewers of the program had called the Urban Institute to protest. But nothing was said directly to me by any of my co-workers.

Living in Chevy Chase was quite delightful. We had lovely neighbors and many neighborhood amenities, such as a country club within walking distance, nice parks, and great shopping. Being among the very few blacks in Chevy Chase taught me a lesson about racial relationships. Living in a corner house, adjacent to busy Jones Bridge Road, prompted a Saturday chore of picking up trash that people discarded from passing cars. One Saturday, while doing that, an elderly white neighbor approached me to ask me whether, when I completed my tasks, I would be interested in working that afternoon in his yard. I told him very nicely that I would be spending that afternoon putting the final touches on my PhD dissertation. The man's face turned red with embarrassment, and he apologized profusely.

Some blacks might have been insulted by the offer and charged the man with racism. But I realized that the man was a Bayesian (Sir Thomas Bayes, the father of probability theory), meaning that if a black person was spotted in Chevy Chase, picking up trash, the overwhelming probability was that he was a worker as opposed to a homeowner. Playing racial odds doesn't make one a racist.

Connie encountered a similar incident. Despite my admonitions to the contrary, she would occasionally hitchhike. One day, when she was going downtown to meet me after work, she walked the short distance from our house to the bus stop on Connecticut Avenue. As she waited for the bus, she was offered a ride by a black woman who turned out to be a domestic servant employed in Chevy Chase. In the ensuing conversation, the woman asked Connie, "Don't you hate working for these cheap white people?" Connie replied that she didn't work for any white people; she lived in Chevy Chase. After they rode in silence for a few more blocks, the domestic told Connie that she was only going as far as Chevy Chase

Circle—not all the way into the city, as she'd originally said—so she was in effect kicking Connie out of the car.

Connie's incident shows that there are black Bayesians as well as white Bayesians. It's by no means unusual for people to use an easy-to-observe characteristic such as race as a proxy for a harder-to-observe characteristic that can include residence, SAT score, or basketball proficiency. On the other hand, one does not have to be a stupid Bayesian. I might spot a green person walking down the street. I might guess that he's from Mars, but before I walk up to him and accuse him of being a Martian, it would be smart of me to gather more information.

Linking Up with Tom Sowell

About six months after my arrival at the Urban Institute, there was talk of establishing a minority-research project. I was invited to several meetings to discuss the idea. A number of names were proposed as project director. Several were political activists. I made the argument that if the people making the hiring decision were serious, and wanted to avoid the kinds of problems that had arisen on college campuses in connection with black studies programs, the person appointed should be a respected academic scholar. I proposed Dr. Thomas Sowell and made a strong argument that he be selected over some other names bandied about. Reginald Brown, a black man, who was an associate director at the institute, gave my suggestion strong backing.

I first met Thomas Sowell in the summer of 1969, when he came to UCLA as a visiting professor to teach his specialty, the history of economic thought. His employment at UCLA is a story in itself. At that time, activist students were demonstrating against the Vietnam War and racial injustice. Their demands for countering the latter included the university hiring more black professors. UCLA's economics department came in for considerable vitriol. It was seen as conservative and therefore, in the eyes of some, racist.

I doubt whether conservative is the proper description of faculty sentiment; sympathetic to free markets is more accurate. UCLA, along with the University of Virginia, was known as a farm team of the University of

Chicago, the home of such distinguished free-market economists such as Nobel Laureates Milton Friedman, George Stigler, and Gary Becker. I have never found evidence that any of those scholars were racist.

In any event, Professor William Allen, chairman of the economics department at UCLA, was a witty, cantankerous person who didn't suffer fools kindly and who had no sympathy for activist threats and demands. His sharp tongue and wit angered both activists and administrators on campus. Some of this anger was expressed by the placement of a small bomb outside his office. The bomb didn't create much of an explosion, but it did cause minor smoke damage.

After considerable administration pressure, William Allen asked Professor Friedman, who was on the Chicago faculty, whether he had any black students whom he might recommend as faculty candidates. Friedman, puzzled, replied that he didn't understand Allen's question. He told Allen that he understood that his former student Thomas Sowell had already been offered and accepted a visiting professorship appointment at UCLA for the 1969 summer semester.

Professor Allen had hired Tom Sowell without having any idea that he was black. Both Allen and Sowell are students of the history of economic thought. Sowell had done path-blazing research on economists Jean Baptiste Say and Sismonde de Sismondi—work that Allen had read and admired. Sowell was offered the visiting professorship position, sight unseen, by way of telephone conversations and an exchange of letters. Race had nothing to do with his being hired and later being offered a full-time position as associate professor of economics at UCLA, one of the top economics departments in the nation. That set of facts refutes allegations that Sowell benefited from affirmative-action hiring.

I became acquainted with Professor Sowell—and established a friendship that lasts to this day—when he joined the UCLA faculty as associate professor in September 1969. Having finished my own studies by the time he arrived, I never had the opportunity to take his course. But we socialized together, and Connie and I joined him and his wife on several occasions for dinners and drinks. In March 1971, Tom called me to say that he had just received a royalty check from his book publisher and wanted to take me to a downtown Los Angeles big-screen theater to see the first Ali-Frazier fight. We were both disappointed that Ali lost.

In the summer of 1972, Tom was hired as the project director for the Urban Institute's Ethnic Minorities Research Project. The ultimate uniqueness of his approach to ethnic research was that he refused to focus only on blacks, as was customary in those days. Studying other racial and ethnic groups in other places led him to challenge some of the unwarranted though conventional assumptions about blacks, particularly the impact of racial discrimination. The project yielded a collection of works, published with the title *American Ethnic Groups*, that launched Tom on a number of other significant investigations of ethnic populations in America and abroad.

Shortly after Sowell's arrival, I joined his group, and I wound up finishing my dissertation later that year as well as doing my own research on minority issues. One of my resulting articles, "Why the Poor Pay More: An Alternative Explanation," published in the *Social Science Quarterly* in 1973, was the subject of my dissertation; and another, "Some Hard Questions on Minority Businesses," appeared in the *Negro Educational Review* a year later.

It was a delight working with Tom. I fondly recall our lunches spent playing chess, although I don't recall winning any matches. It turned out that he was just as controversial at the Urban Institute as I was, maybe even more so.

Back to Philadelphia

In early 1973, Temple University's economics department chairman, Professor Louis Harms, called to ask me whether I'd be interested in giving a paper and discussing the possibility of a teaching position in his department. Though I longed to get back to teaching, I had never considered Temple University, much less returning to Philadelphia. I accepted the invitation in large measure because it afforded Connie and me a free trip to visit our families.

After the trip, the interviews, and a job offer, I began to think of Temple as a serious possibility for me. One thing I wanted to make sure of was that I wouldn't be an affirmative-action hire. I specifically asked Professor Harms whether he was under any pressure to hire a black faculty member. He said no, but admitted that my being black was an unavoidable plus for the department; at that point, it had a single black member, a West Indian. I told Professor Harms that I would take him at his word. But if it turned out he was being untruthful, I would quit the very day I discovered that—even if it was in the middle of a semester. I have always found a hiring on the basis of race, ethnicity, or sex demeaning and offensive.

In September 1973, Connie and I, as well as her niece, Kelly, who was living with us in order to attend better schools, moved to Devon, Pennsylvania, one of the communities on the Philadelphia suburbs' posh "Main Line," and I started teaching at Temple University. Temple is located at Broad and Montgomery Street in North Philadelphia, a mere ten blocks from the Richard Allen housing projects, where I grew up. Connie sometimes joked that I had never truly made it out of the slums of North Philadelphia.

Most of my Temple colleagues were on the liberal end of the political spectrum, but not the crazy liberals I encountered on other college campuses. A prime example of the craziness occurred at the University of Massachusetts/Amherst, where I interviewed before deciding on Temple. I found the prospect of working at "UMass" attractive because its faculty included Professor Simon Rottenberg, whose work on occupational licensing, minimum wages, and other labor economics topics I had read and admired. But I was not at all prepared for what I encountered when I visited the school.

I presented my "job" paper and responded to faculty and graduate students' questions and comments. As is usually the case, a candidate is taken to dinner or a reception. I was taken to both, and remarkably, no faculty member other than the department chairman *attended* both. As it turned out, the department was sharply divided along political lines. The attendees at the reception were leftists, some of them members of the Union for Radical Political Economists (URPE), a Marxist and avowedly anti-capitalist organization. The faculty members at the dinner were unflatteringly called by the leftist types "mathematical economists," which is a misnomer; they were conservative or free-market economists. As for Professor Rottenberg, he was everything but a mathematical economist.

At the leftist reception, in the course of conversation and drinks, one of the faculty members asked me what I thought about the relationship between capitalism and slavery. My response to him and others, who were standing near to listen to my answer, was that to my knowledge, slavery has existed everywhere in the world and under every political and economic system; so slavery was by no means unique to capitalism or the United States. Not satisfied with my answer, the questioner asked, "How do you feel about the enslavement of your ancestors?"

They were all shocked by my response; it was a party stopper. I started off by saying that slavery is one of the most despicable abuses of human rights. But the enslavement of my ancestors is history, and one of the immutable facts of history is that nothing can be done to change it. I could have let the matter rest. But I went further to tell them that I, Walter E. Williams, have benefited enormously from the horrible suffering of my ancestors. After a few gasps and shocked expressions, I explained: assuming my birth in any event, my wealth and personal liberties are greater having been born in the United States rather than in any African country.

I then asked, "How is it that I came to be born in the United States, as opposed to some poverty-ridden country in Africa?" I answered my own question, telling them that I and millions of other blacks wound up being born here because of slavery. I attempted to assuage the shock of the audience gathered around me by telling them that to morally condemn a practice, in this case slavery, does not require one to deny its beneficial effects.

The next few minutes were uncomfortable. Thankfully, one of the "mathematical economists" showed up to drive the chairman and me to dinner. Relating this story at that event helped make the conversation quite pleasant and interesting.

Next morning, stopping by the chairman's office en route to the airport, I was asked for the names of references. I declined, telling him that his department was not for me. I might have added that I didn't want to lose credibility with my references; I was certainly thinking that.

There was another job interview of note—at the University of Cincinnati. I would have been happy with an appointment there, because the faculty included Professor Alfred Kuhn, whom I admired; as an undergraduate, I'd been influenced by his book, *The Study of Society: A Unified Approach*. The Cincinnati department chairman picked me up at the airport. We had a nice chat on the way to the campus and my first meeting, with the head of the university's affirmative-action office. After a half hour of conversation, I was taken to the office of the African-studies department chairman.

When the economics department chairman returned to escort me to lunch, I asked him whether it was standard procedure to schedule candidates for appointment in the economics department meetings with the affirmative-action and African studies people. He answered, with embarrassment, no; but he wanted to make me feel comfortable by being introduced to the black members of the campus community. I sarcastically told him that I was becoming quite uncomfortable, because I hadn't met the economists among the campus community.

The chairman, whose name I've forgotten, was a gentleman and a respectable economist. I'm guessing that he was under pressure to hire a black person and had been advised how to make one feel at ease at Cincinnati. Alas, he tried the strategy on the wrong person. I left the campus with mixed feelings. I wanted to work there, and I liked the city of Cincinnati. But I wasn't going to be their affirmative-action hire.

Upon returning home, I telephoned the chairman to tell him that if the department were to vote to make me an offer, I wouldn't accept it, so he should not bother with all the paperwork. That experience prompted me to raise the issue with chairmen at Temple and later George Mason University. My question: were they under pressure to hire a black?

Controversy at Temple

Shortly after I started teaching in Philadelphia, I was invited to lunch by one of the senior economics professors, George Rohrlich. In the course of our conversation, Professor Rohrlich explained that he was having academic problems with many of the black students who enrolled in his introductory courses, and he wondered whether I might have any helpful suggestions. He said that the blacks wrote poorly, often didn't hand in assignments on time, and in some cases fell asleep during class.

Surprised by that complaint, I asked him how he handled the problem. He said he tried to take into consideration their poor schooling and experiences with racial discrimination. "That," I said, "was not my question. At the end of the semester, you must assign grades. What do you do?" Remarkably, Rohrlich said that if the black students attend class every day and look like they're taking notes, he gives them a C grade.

I asked, "Do you know what you're saying and to whom you're saying it?" Puzzled, he asked me to explain. I told him that his actions didn't differ that much from the case of an English teacher who happened to have a dog in class: "If, during the course of the semester, the dog stood on his hind legs and said, 'You not 'posed ta do dat,' you'd give the damned dog an A. Why? Because a dog isn't expected to talk in the first place, so no matter what it says and how, the result is laudable." I went on to tell him that there was no more effective way to mislead black students and discredit whatever legitimate achievements they might make than giving them phony grades and ultimately fraudulent diplomas.

Professor Rohrlich was not at all unkind; he was a gentleman, a scholar, and a person truly concerned with the plight of minorities. He himself was an Austrian Jew who escaped Hitler's rampage. His treatment of his black students demonstrated just how much compassion can cloud the mind of an otherwise intelligent, kind, and honest person. To his credit, he thanked me and said he'd never thought of his actions in that light. Still, I haven't any idea whether our conversation had a real impact on him.

Another racial matter arose during my first year at Temple. Black students had demanded the addition of a "black economics" course. Some of my colleagues were seriously entertaining the idea. When they sought my opinion, I asked them what—if anything—theoretical can one say about systematic differences in the economic behavior of blacks compared to whites? Are there black postulates and white postulates of such behavior? My colleagues had no answers that made any sense.

During one discussion, I offered my fellow professors full and general amnesty and pardon for both their own grievances and those of their forebears against my people. I told them that my reason for doing so was to assuage their feelings of guilt so they could stop acting like fools. I asked what they would do if some of Temple University's Irish or Italian students demanded a course in Irish or Italian economics. I answered the question for them: "You'd dismiss those students as idiots and throw them out of your offices. Why wouldn't you do the same with a similarly silly demand from black students?" It couldn't have been because they saw logic and merit in *black* students demanding such a course but none in their Irish and Italian counterparts doing the same. One possibility, of course, is that the professors feared accusations of racism if they were to summarily reject the demands of black students. The other possibility was worse: their intelligence had been so compromised by feelings of guilt that they saw academic merit in a course on purported black economics. Fortunately, such an economics course was never offered.

I'd occasionally lose patience with some of my liberal colleagues, for example, when I had had it with one super-liberal. He was a very nice guy but also very naïve, and he was spouting guilt-motivated nonsense to me. I suggested that he cure himself of guilt for what his ancestors did to mine by stealing a car, getting arrested, and then getting sentenced for a year or so at Philadelphia's Graterford Prison. I told him that by the time my "brothers" got finished with him, and had him wearing panties and makeup and carrying a pocketbook, he'd be happy about what his ancestors did to mine. My response might have been a bit strong and unprofessional, but it brought a reward: he hardly spoke to me again.

Professor Lynn Holmes was one of the colleagues with whom I had many conversations and, together with our wives, shared social events. We were friends. One day, he casually volunteered that I shouldn't blame racism for any faculty resentment toward me. He laughingly added, "Walter, even if you were white, people wouldn't like you."

Early in 1974, prompted by my own experiences and those told to me by faculty and students, I wrote a memo to the professors at Temple's business school (which also housed its economics department) titled "Fraudulent Grades"—that is, awarding them to black students. (See pages 100–101.) The immediate prompt for the memo was an angry office visit by a black student who had submitted a term paper for my urban economics course. A secondary prompt was the luncheon conversation with Professor Rorhlich described previously.

The student had submitted a term paper with little coherent thought, poor grammar, footnotes at the tops of pages, and many misspellings. I assigned a grade of F. She argued that she'd received an unfair grade and offered what she considered to be proof: an identical paper she had turned in as an assignment for a class she took a previous semester. The other professor, who was white, gave her an A-minus with complimentary notes in the margins—"keep up the good work" and "good point." She stomped out of my office in anger when I suggested that what the professor might have had in mind was that it was good work for a black student—because he didn't expect any better.

What made the confrontation sadder was that it never occurred to her that turning in the identical paper for different classes is not an accepted academic practice, in fact, worthy of a failing grade in and of itself. By my own choice, I never taught the urban economics class again. Most of the students who enrolled in it were majors in journalism, education, communication, and other "soft" disciplines who had little experience with analytical thought and rigorous demands.

Somehow the memo to my colleagues in the business school got into the hands of a *Philadelphia Inquirer* reporter, who called to interview me. The interview, photo and all, landed on the front page with the headline: "Racism? Temple Professor Opposes Easy Grades for Blacks." (See pages 102–103.)

The newspaper story brought a mixed response. The *Inquirer* reporter wrote that Seymour Wolfbein, dean of the business school, said he "admired Williams' 'guts' in writing the memo but felt that any leniency towards blacks occurred in lower-level courses and did not result in

TEMPLE UNIVERSITY
SCHOOL OF BUSINESS ADMINISTRATION
PHILADELPHIA, PENNSYLVANIA 19122

DEPARTMENT OF ECONOMICS

January 4, 1974

MEMORANDUM

TO: Faculty, School of Business Administration

FROM: Dr. Walter E. Williams

SUBJECT: Fraudulent Grades

It has come to my attention through several sources that some minority students are being treated differently in the School of Business than are their majority counterparts. The allegations and rumors assert that in some classes minority students are receiving grades higher than that merited by academic performance. The alleged reasons for this behavior on behalf of my colleagues varies from those having to do with fear to those having to do with "compensatory" treatment. Aside from moral indignations that could be made, I have some observations to make on an academic process that I fear is widespread on Temple campus:

1. A significant part of the problem has to do with "open admissions" policy which brings relatively unqualified minority students to campus. One of the most insistent arguments given for special admissions for blacks is that standard mental tests are culturally biased. While there is evidence that mental tests underestimate the mental ability of low-income people in general, such tests may not underestimate success in college which requires many attributes besides native mental ability. The predictive validity of these tests (e.g., SAT) is not a matter of philosophical stances but a matter of empirical testing. Successful college performance is not solely a matter of raw native intelligence but, in addition, it is a result of years of accumulation and development of mental habits which cannot be readily developed through standard remedial programs.

2. Differential treatment and responses to cope with relatively unqualified black students can take several forms. Reduced course loads and remedial courses are one form. Credits given for courses with little content, double standards in grading, incomplete or withdrawal grades given for failing work, and withdrawal from college disguising flunking out of college is another. The first forms of differential treatment has an advantage over the latter mainly because it is open and above board, while the latter is clandestine and dishonest and more importantly harmful to black students and black people.

Source: In the author's possession.

Faculty, School of Business Administration
Dr. Walter E. Williams
Page 2.

    3. Most discussion of double standards focuses on the undermining of
academic standards and completely ignores what these standards do to black
students
        a. The benevolent paternalism of white faculty members tend to generate
            "hustler" attitudes among black students.
        b. Fraudulent grading denies black students measures of their relative
            competency.
        c. It fosters superiority attitudes among white students and tends to
            reinforce stereotypical views held of blacks.
        d. It undermines the effort and merit of those minority students who
            receive honest grades.
        e. Regardless of the _intent_ of double standards in grading, it plays
            into the hands of the most racist elements in our society for there
            is no more effective way of destroying the creditability of academic
            accomplishments by blacks.

    Having made these observations on academic practices in the School of
Business, I recognize that there are those who would defend these practices
by pointing out that white subgroups such as athletes and night school
students may be faced with similar practices. In this connection, I would
just point out that such an argument uses the least reputable white academic
practice as a norm for blacks. Second, whites are not, as blacks are,
operating under the historical stereotype of mental incompetence. Double
standards would seem to reinforce these stereotypes.

    Having made the foregoing observations, allow me to conclude by saying
that as a social scientist I recognize that people (professors) are utility
maximizers and as such will choose among alternative behavioral responses
that which optimizes. In that light, I can intellectually respect the professor
who gives a black student a B when he earns a D because he fears some type
of retaliation. On the other hand the professor who engages in such behavior
motivated by guilt or a passion to compensate for historical inequities finds
only intellectual and human contempt in my heart.

Source: In the author's possession.

The Philadelphia Inquirer

Oldest Daily Newspaper in the United States—Founded 1771

Saturday, January 25, 1975

Daily Home Delivery 25c U

Philadelphia Inquirer / EARNEST S. EDDOWES

Professor Williams accuses colleagues of reverse racism

RACISM?

Temple Professor Opposes Easy Grades for Blacks

By **PAUL JABLOW**
Inquirer Education Writer

A black faculty member at Temple University has accused some of his white colleagues of reverse racism by overly lenient grading of black students.

Walter E. Williams, an assistant professor of economics, said in a memorandum to fellow faculty members at the School of Business Administration that the alleged practice "is clandestine and dishonest and, more importantly, harmful to black students and black people."

Williams, 38, a Philadelphia native who attended Benjamin Franklin High School, said in an interview Friday that he wrote the memo because "somebody has to tell the emperor he has no clothes on."

He said that since he distributed the memo about three weeks ago, he received only slight reaction from his colleagues but that the reaction had been favorable.

Seymour L. Wolfbein, dean of the school, said he admired Williams' "guts" in writing the memo but felt that any leniency toward blacks occurred in lower-level courses and did not result in cheapening a Temple business diploma.

Williams, who has been at Temple for a year and a half, said he had noticed the practice at the business school but felt it was probably more prevalent in other departments of the university. ,

He said he had drawn his conclusions from talks with other faculty members, complaints from white students and occasional personal experiences.

In one such case, he said, a black stu-
(See GRADES on 2-A)

Professor Opposes Leniency for Blacks

GRADES, From 1-A

dent submitted the same paper in his course and another course, although this is not permitted. The other professor, apparently white, gave the paper a B or an A-minus, Williams said. He flunked it.

"I wouldn't have accepted it from a high school junior," he said. "It didn't contain one coherent sentence."

Williams added that at a faculty meeting, he heard a white professor admit that he would give a C to any black student who "appeared to be taking notes."

In his memo, entitled "Fraudulent Grading," Williams charged that the alleged practice:

• Denies black students measures of their relative competency.

• Fosters superiority attitudes among white students and tends to reinforce stereotypical views held by blacks.

• Undermines the effort and merit of those minority students who receive honor grades.

"Regardless of the intent of double standards in grading," he said, "it plays into the hands of the most racist elements in our society for there is no more effective way of destroying the creditability of accomplishments by blacks.

"The alleged reasons for this behavior on behalf of my colleagues varies from those having to do with fear to those having to do with 'compensatory' treatment.

"I can intellectually respect the professor who gives a black student a B when he earns a D because he fears some type of retaliation. On the other hand, the professor who engages in such behavior motivated by guilt or passion to compensate for historical inequities finds only intellectual and human contempt in my heart."

Williams said he believed Temple's virtual "open admissions" policy could work, but only if it devoted more resources to remedial courses and monitored them more stringently.

"It's a good time to start focusing on these things," he said. "We have more common sense now than we had in the 1960's. By 1980, we'll have forgotten about 'affirmative action'."

Williams also supports the use of some standardized tests criticized as culturally biased, because "blacks and minorities don't go out into a culture-free world."

Williams says he is receiving more support for his views among black colleagues than he was in the 1960's but that he had held the same views then.

He said that when he was teaching at a West Coast college, a black student came to him and told him he needed a B in his course to graduate. He told Williams that he wanted to teach in Watts.

Williams says he dismissed the student, stating that "You want to be one more p--- poor teacher in Watts. If you'd said the San Fernando Valley I'd have given you the B."

Source: Paul Jablow, "Racism? Temple Professor Opposes Easy Grades for Blacks," *The Philadelphia Inquirer*, January 25, 1975.

cheapening a Temple business diploma." A few other faculty members complimented me for the stance I was taking, but—probably out of fear of reprisal—they didn't offer anything for quotation.

Shortly after that story appeared, I was invited to address Temple's black faculty and students about the memo. I accepted, and the event turned out to resemble an inquisition. In fact, on several occasions, I sarcastically asked, "Do you think the Constitution's First Amendment guarantee [of free speech] applies to me?" and "Should I have sent you the memo for prior approval?" That inflamed emotions even more.

My most resented comment, which the Inquirer reported, was this: "He said when he was teaching at a West Coast college [Cal State], a black student came to him and told him that he needed a B in his course in order to graduate. He told Williams that he wanted to teach in Watts. Williams says he dismissed the student, stating that 'You want to be one more piss-poor teacher in Watts. If you'd said San Fernando Valley I'd have given you the B.'" (At the time, the late 1960s, schools in Watts were predominantly black and those in "the Valley" predominantly white.)

The controversy did not bother me one bit, and it eventually died down. One factor in the dying down was the fact that, in the summer of 1975, my wife and I, along with Devyn, our newborn daughter, left for Stanford University's Hoover Institution, where I had been appointed a National Fellow for one year.

During my tenure at Temple, I did make efforts to assist black students academically. For example, I conducted after-hours tutorials in calculus. My counsel to one black student, Warren Whatley, caused a bit of concern among my colleagues. Whatley was taking the PhD-level microeconomic theory course I taught. On all graded work, such as problem sets and examinations, he scored the highest or second-highest grade in a class of 30 or so students, the rest of whom were white. At the end of the semester, I invited him to my office. I told him that he was among the brightest students, black or white, that I had taught. I suggested that if he were going to spend time earning a PhD, he'd benefit by transferring to a university that had an economics program with a better reputation than Temple's. He acted on my advice, and was admitted to Stanford.

Connie "infanticipating," 1974.

When several of my colleagues discovered that it was I who encouraged and assisted Warren Whatley's transfer, they were a bit irritated and chided me for helping one of our better graduate students leave the Temple program. I told them I felt it was my responsibility to counsel a student in his own best interests, even if that conflicted with what might be in the best interest of the department.

It wasn't a racial matter for me. Many years later, I made the identical suggestion in the case of Laura Inglis, a white George Mason University student, who was the brightest undergraduate student I've ever taught. She was a home-schooled high school senior when she took my intermediate microeconomics course and got the second-highest grade. (I found out later that she'd scored 1575/1600 on the SATs.) I therefore recommended that Inglis choose an institution more challenging than George Mason.

She didn't take my advice. The dean of the College of Arts and Sciences, Daniele Struppa, found out about my recommendation. Instead of becoming bitter, the dean joined me as Laura's co-advisors, and we made sure that she had access to George Mason's most challenging courses, including those at the graduate level.

A Year at Hoover

At the end of the 1975 spring semester, I took a leave of absence to accept the one-year appointment at the Hoover Institution on War, Peace and Revolution. The position involved no teaching obligations, and I spent the entire time doing research and attending lectures—as well as, at night and on weekends, adapting to fatherhood.

The Hoover Institution was very conducive to thinking, writing, and doing research. The administrators gave me ample computer time and a research assistant, as well as a very nice office. Interactions with such Hoover residents as Aaron Director, Gary Becker, Milton Friedman, and Edward Teller, along with visiting scholars and guest lecturers, made for a lively and productive academic environment. I especially profited from conversations and lunches with Director, a very distinguished econo-mist. In discussing our common field, it was nearly impossible to say something to him that he agreed was 100 percent correct. He'd always respond, "Have you thought of this?" or "That's right most of the time, but. . . ." I'm sure that had I declared that two plus two is four, he would have pointed out an exception I should consider.

One of my research projects was to start a study commissioned by the Joint Economic Committee of Congress, later published under the title "Youth and Minority Unemployment." It examined the effects of the minimum-wage law on youth and minority unemployment as well as the racially discriminatory effects of the Davis-Bacon Act of 1931. During the 1970s, criticism of the minimum-wage law was far less common and more controversial than it is today, and initially the Joint Economic Committee refused to publish my report—a matter I will dis-cuss later. In addition to that study, I managed to collect material for a book that I would complete several years later.

Among the fringe benefits at Hoover was the location of my office, next to that of Edward Teller, the physicist often called the father of the

Connie and
Devyn by the San
Francisco Bay,
December 1975.

hydrogen bomb. I'm fascinated by—though not competent in—that
scientific field, particularly subatomic physics. Being next to Teller's
office allowed me to bug him with occasional questions. He'd answer
them and suggest books or articles to read, albeit grumpily. In addition,
through jogging, I met a few members of the Stanford Linear Accelerator
Center. I visited the center a few times and became fascinated by their
research, although Teller sometimes (again grumpily) criticized it as
"particle proliferation."

Another source of pleasure during the year at Stanford was my adjust-
ment to being a father to a lovely daughter. Because I am an early riser,
typically around four o'clock, my office day started around six in the
morning. Most afternoons, therefore, I'd arrive home around 4:00 P.M.,
just after Connie had fed Devyn. Nearly every evening, I carried her on

a child's seat on my bike along Stanford's many bike paths. After the ride, we'd take a bath together, and after that she was often asleep by the time I was halfway through reading a bedtime story. After Devyn began to walk, we spent many early evenings at playgrounds.

All of this was more than fun; it also gave Connie a break. If she was having a frustrating day, she could at least look forward to the late afternoon, when I'd take over the child-care duties for the rest of the day.

Beginning a Public Life

During the summer of 1976, we returned to our home in Devon, Pennsylvania, and I resumed teaching at Temple that fall. Looking back at my time at the Hoover Institution, it was just about the most productive year in my professional career. But that career was about to add another dimension.

During the fall of 1976, I met Jay Parker, director of the Washington, D.C.-based Lincoln Institute, a black think tank that was just getting off the ground. He invited me there to give a talk on my still-unpublished congressional report on youth and minority unemployment. In the audience at the talk were Senators Samuel Ichiye Hayakawa and Orrin Hatch. They also attended a May 1977 reception for me that Jay Parker sponsored in Alexandria, Virginia. In the course of conversation that evening, I told the senators that the Joint Economic Committee refused to publish my study on the minimum wage and the Davis-Bacon Act. My criticism of the minimum-wage law and the Davis-Bacon Act, I said, were probably the reason.

Shortly after I returned to Philadelphia, I received a call from a committee staff member telling me that the report was under review for publication. Senators Hayakawa and Hatch had contacted the committee to demand that either my commissioned study be published or a persuasive explanation be offered for why it would remain on the shelf. After some haggling and editorial concessions on my part, the work finally appeared in mid-1977. (I acceded to some of the politically motivated editing because the Hoover Institution offered to publish an unexpurgated version.)

My controversial minimum-wage study helped launch the more public side of my professional career. My study concluded that minimum wages caused high rates of teenage unemployment, particularly that of minority teenagers. The study also showed that the Davis-Bacon Act, requiring high prevailing wages on federally financed or assisted construction projects, had explicit racist motivations expressed by congressmen and senators during its legislative debates in 1931. Publication of the study led to numerous radio and television interviews, the attendant publicity to my being invited to lecture at colleges across the country. The lectures were titled "Government-Sanctioned Restraints that Reduce Economic Opportunities for Minorities," and most of them took place under the auspices of the Intercollegiate Studies Institute.

Another aspect of my public life stemmed from a weekly newspaper column I began writing. After I returned from my year at the Hoover Institution, I got a message from Alfred Morris, who had recently become president of the *Philadelphia Tribune*, the nation's oldest black newspaper. Morris said he wanted to partly change the newspaper's focus by including some economics coverage and bringing aboard a conservative writer. I agreed to write a weekly, sometimes twice-weekly, column. As it turned out, readers were clipping the column and sending it to people in other cities.

In 1980, I met Ed Grimsley, then editorial page editor of the *Richmond Times-Dispatch*. Mr. Grimsley, who had been reading the column, told me that considering the small readership, I was wasting my time writing for a paper like the *Philadelphia Tribune*. I ought, he said, to become syndicated.

The Heritage Foundation, a conservative, Washington-based think tank, was just launching its Heritage Features Syndicate. Grimsley promised that if Heritage Features syndicated my column, the Richmond paper would subscribe to it. That was almost 30 years ago, and the *Times-Dispatch* continues to carry the column on a weekly basis.

In 1991, I joined Creators Syndicate as part of its friendly takeover of Heritage Features. My weekly column is carried today in more than 140 newspapers and on numerous websites, and it is occasionally translated for Latin American newspapers and sites.

While I continued to teach at Temple University, I frequently traveled to Washington to participate in meetings and to testify before both houses of Congress on topics that ranged from minimum-wage laws and the Davis-Bacon Act to poverty and welfare. I gave speeches to organizations such as the U.S. Chamber of Commerce and Associated Builders and Contractors, as well as to think tanks like the Heritage and Right to Work foundations and the American Enterprise Institute. In 1978, under a Rockefeller Foundation grant, I spent a summer as a resident scholar at Heritage, to start a research project on occupational licensure that would later become an important part of my first book, *The State against Blacks*. Those activities led to numerous requests for radio, television, and newspaper interviews, and often generated considerable reporter hostility.

There's another story of note about my teaching experiences at Temple University. When I returned from the Hoover Institution, my duties included teaching the PhD microeconomics seminar and serving on the PhD examination committee. Having a black student in my graduate class was rare. During the first few class meetings, some of the whites would ask searching questions that sometimes required that I go through a mathematical proof.

Although I never suggested this to the students, it was my impression—not born of paranoia, I trust—that they were testing my credentials, checking to see whether I was competent in my subject. I'd simply answer their question and move on. After a few classes that kind of questioning stopped. In the rare cases when the class did include a black student, who might have sensed what was going on, I could almost read a sigh of relief on his face. Maybe he said to himself, with relief, "The brother could answer the question!"

When a black undergraduate student visited my office to talk—and sometimes mildly complain that if I weren't so demanding in my classes maybe more black students would enroll in them—I would raise the above point. In one of those conversations, I said that I love subatomic physics and would love to teach it, but black people can't afford to have me do so. I added that because of talented people such as Jackie Robinson and Wilt Chamberlain, I can now play professional baseball or basketball. That is, in those sports and many others, black people can now "afford" incompetents. We can't yet afford them in physics, but I look forward to the day when we can.

Our discussions always ended amicably with the students telling me, "We see where you're coming from."

To the "Old Dominion" and George Mason

In late 1979, Professor William Snavely, chairman of George Mason University's economics department, asked whether I'd be interested in a teaching position there and invited me to the campus for an interview. I accepted his invitation. Although George Mason was at that time a little-known institution of modest distinction in northern Virginia, I found its economics faculty congenial and accepting of my free-market principles. I had the same conversation with Professor Snavely that I had had with Professor Harms at Temple, namely about whether he was under any pressure to hire a black faculty member. Snavely assured me that he wasn't, and I thought he was being honest. Some twenty years later, I discovered that was not the case. The revelation occurred during a short speech that he, by this time in his eighties and long retired from the faculty, gave during a gathering at the university.

On that occasion, the former chairman recounted some of what he considered his successes as head of the department. One of those was to recruit Karen Vaughn and later me so as to have more women and minority faculty members, adding how pleased the administration had been. Because George Mason's economics department had a conservative/free-market reputation, other faculty members and administrators might have seen the department as racist or racially insensitive. Karen Vaughn, who had been hired a couple of years earlier, told me recently that she had heard of no affirmative-action pressure to hire me. She also informed me that even if there had been, hiring me would not have satisfied anyone because I didn't turn out to be the "right" kind of black, that is, politically and economically liberal.

In any case, George Mason offered me a position on the economics faculty, beginning in the fall of 1980. I asked that the appointment be made on a one-year *visiting* basis so that the department and I could get to know and evaluate each other. The position appealed to me in a number of ways. I was at that point traveling from Pennsylvania to Washington three or four times a month. George Mason University is not far from downtown Washington. Thus, I could kill two birds with one stone: I could teach and keep up with the new Washington-based aspect of my life; in addition, I was being paid a slightly higher salary. When I returned to my home in Devon, I would be finished with teaching and the public side of my life, and could dedicate most of the remaining time to my family and writing.

CHAPTER SIX

Teaching and Preaching

WHEN I ACCEPTED MY PROFESSORSHIP at George Mason University, I never thought I'd be working there thirty years later. For one thing, doing so required commuting 163 miles between my Pennsylvania home and Fairfax, Virginia.

For me, a primary attraction of George Mason's economics department was the character of my colleagues. They accepted me as an economist, not as a *black* economist. They were all friendly, and we shared the same philosophy of equality before the law and limited government—that is, libertarian values. In addition, I was simply given teaching assignments and otherwise left alone—a very important consideration.

At the outset, I taught on Tuesday and Thursday mornings. That enabled me to leave my Devon residence very early Tuesday morning for a 7:30 class, followed by another at 10:00. Aside from maintaining office hours, I was free the rest of the time to engage in whatever Washington activities came up. On Thursdays, after class, I drove to Devon. My initial home in Fairfax was a cheap hotel that I occupied two nights a week.

In Washington, I delivered a speech at the U.S. Chamber of Commerce. That's where I met Dr. Richard Rahn, the organization's vice president and chief economist. When Richard found out that I was spending my nights locally at the hotel, he graciously invited me to live with him in his spacious house in Great Falls, Virginia. I accepted, and we became very good friends. We were roommates for more than six years, until Richard married Peggy Noonan, who was President Reagan's chief speechwriter.

Although they both wanted me to stay, I decided it was best to leave married people alone, particularly newlyweds. Connie and I decided to purchase a townhouse adjacent to George Mason for my two or three nights a week in the Washington area.

Richard Rahn's work at the U.S. Chamber of Commerce brought him in contact with many congressmen, senators, and other government officials, and through him I met some of them. The early 1980s were heady times in the nation's capitol. Ronald Reagan had just been elected the fortieth president. Richard, along with Art Laffer, Paul Craig Roberts, and others at the U.S. Chamber of Commerce were heavily involved with the White House and Congress, most notably in making the case for the tax cuts that would become known as the Kemp-Roth bill. Reagan had campaigned on the promise of cuts, and he supported the Kemp-Roth bill (officially the Economic Recovery Tax Act of 1981) that drastically slashed marginal tax rates. Despite the gloomy predictions of many politicians and economists, the measure led to a dramatic turnaround in the U.S. economy and cut the inflation rate from 13 percent at the beginning of the 1980s to 4 percent when Reagan left office.

I wrote columns supporting President Reagan's domestic agenda of cutting taxes, deregulating the economy, reforming the welfare system, and limiting government involvement in our lives. My position was way out of step with the average black person—and just about every black politician and civil rights advocate. As a result, I was interviewed on radio and television quite extensively, often with hostility, about the effects of the president's policies on the nation and blacks, and on the poor in particular.

Shortly after Ronald Reagan's 1980 election, Thomas Sowell invited me to participate in a conference he was organizing. Titled "Black Alternatives," it took place in San Francisco and was later dubbed by the media the Fairmont Conference. (It also attracted the name "the meeting of black Republicans," although neither Tom nor I are Republicans.) Quite a few of the attendees were Democrats, and at least two were officials in the Democratic Party (Percy Sutton and Charles V. Hamilton, who co-authored Black Power with Stokely Carmichael). Other participants included Nobel Laureate Milton Friedman; Stanford University economist Michael Boskin; Tony Brown, host of TV's *Tony Brown's Journal*; Clarence Thomas, then an aide to Senator John Danforth; and Ed Meese, who had been chief of staff when Reagan was California's governor and who later became U.S. attorney general.

The objective of the conference was to bring together people of different races (though most of the participants were black) and different opinions to present papers and to discuss problems that confront black Americans as well as the public policies that might alleviate the problems.

The conference proceeded in a civilized, non-rancorous fashion without charges of Uncle Tomism and selling out. In fact, the gathering proved so harmonious that some in the media termed it as a "love fest." The proceedings were later published as *The Fairmont Papers: Black Alternatives Conference.**

Attacks on Black Conservatives

It might be difficult nowadays to comprehend the nastiness of the time. To give readers the flavor, I'll cite a few examples:

◆ NAACP General Counsel Thomas Atkins, upon hearing that Reagan was considering appointing Tom Sowell as head of the Council of Economic Advisors, declared that Sowell "would play the same kind of role which historically house niggers played for the plantation owners."

◆ Syndicated columnist Carl Rowan said, "If you give Thomas [Sowell] a little flour on his face, you'd think you had [former Ku Klux Klan leader] David Duke."

◆ A Rowan column in a September 1981 *Washington Post* read in part, "These are times when I want to ask the Lord to deliver us back to the days of Stepin Fetchit, Aunt Jemima and Uncle Tom. The old-style black, illiterate, obsequious 'handkerchief heads' were an

---

*Thomas Sowell, *The Fairmont Papers: Black Alternatives Conference* (San Francisco: Institute for Contemporary Studies, 1981).

embarrassment, but they were harmless compared with the 'educated' blacks who are now darlings of the far Right." If that weren't enough, Rowan added, "Vidkun Quisling, in his collaboration with the Nazis, surely did not do as much damage to the Norwegians as Sowell is doing to the most helpless of black Americans. Sowell is giving aid and comfort to America's racists and to those who, in the name of conservatism and frugality, are taking the food out of the mouths of black children, consigning hundreds of thousands of black teenagers to joblessness and hopelessness, and making government a party to at least the partial resegregation of America."

What prompted that tirade, Rowan wrote, was "watching Thomas Sowell on a TV interview dishing out bull under the label of scholarship." In the columnist's eyes, the "bull" was Sowell's comments about the unemployment effects of the minimum-wage law, particularly on black youth. Rowan was obviously oblivious to the broad consensus among academic economists that the minimum-wage law discriminates against the employment of low-skilled workers, who are disproportionately black teenagers. Indeed, a 1976 survey by the American Economic Association found that 90 percent of its members agreed that increasing the minimum wage increases unemployment among the young and unskilled.[*] A subsequent survey, in 1990, found 80 percent of economists agreeing with the proposition that increases in the minimum wage cause unemployment among the youth and low skilled.[†]

There's an interesting twist to Carl Rowan's attack on Sowell. In September 1983, I delivered a luncheon address to a gathering in Cleveland sponsored by the Ashbrook Memorial Center for Public Affairs at Ashland University. My address was titled "Government Intervention and Individual Freedom." A couple of weeks later, The [Cleveland] Plain Dealer's George Jordan wrote a "report" about my luncheon address

---

[*] J.R. Kearl et al., "What Economists Think," American Economic Review, Vol. 69, No. 2 (May 1979): 30.

[†] Richard M. Alston, J.R. Kearl, and Michael B. Vaughn, "Is There Global Economic Consensus? Is There a Consensus among Economists in the 1990s?" American Economic Review, Vol. 82, No. 2 (May 1992): 204.

Best friend Tom Sowell, visiting us in 1984.

captioned "Williams Speaks for the Oppressors." It began, "At times I wish the Lord would deliver me back to the days of Stepin Fetchit, Aunt Jemima and Uncle Tom. The old-style black illiterate 'handkerchief heads' were an embarrassment, but they were harmless in comparison to 'educated' blacks like economist Walter E. Williams, a darling of the far Right. . . . Williams is a butter-tongued apologist for the new oppressors of the most helpless black Americans." Jordan added, "I could never really get angry at the old Stepin Fetchits and Aunt Jemimas for they were really uneducated and simply practicing the art of survival. But I have only contempt for people like Williams."

It's obvious that George Jordan plagiarized, virtually word for word, parts of the Carl Rowan column quoted just above. But the plot thickens. Some several months after Jordan's attack, I was invited back to Cleveland for a meeting with the editors and several executives of The

Williams speaks for the oppressors

By George E. Jordan

At times I wish the Lord would deliver me back to the days of Stepin Fetchit, Aunt Jemima and Uncle Tom.

The old-style black, illiterate "hankerchief heads" were an embarrassment, but they were harmless in comparison to "educated" blacks like economist Walter E. Williams, a darling of the far-right.

I can't recall the last time I was as disgusted as when Williams came to town Sept. 27 selling his bill of goods about the virtues of free enterprise and getting the federal government off the backs of people.

Williams has the right to be a conservative and to articulate the position of the far right, and to get paid for his services. Fine.

But I must also exercise my right to say that Williams is a butter-tongued apologist for the new oppressors of the most helpless black Americans.

Williams, an adviser in the early days of the Reagan administration, has be.. trotting around the country the last thr..' years promoting laissez-faire governm..t. He argues that the nation's free enterprise system has been undermined by do-gooders interested in redistributing wealth to the less fortunate. That task, he says, should be left to private charity.

As a college professor who likes to quote this study and that study, Williams offers some good arguments, but they hint at intellectual dishonesty and opportunism.

I nearly choked on my ice cream about six months ago when I stumbled upon Williams on my television selling Reaganism on the Christian Broadcast Network.

I was dismayed at his attempt during the interview to demean the role of the federal government in lifting black Americans towards equality and dignity. But what galled me most about Williams was his refusal to admit that he was helped by the civil rights movement. He figures that if there had been an affirmative action program when he got

his first teaching job, some woman would have gotten his post.

He just couldn't shape his lips to say that real progress in the South did not come until the passage of the Civil Rights Act of 1964. I know that my struggle to become a journalist was easier because of the work of the NAACP, the Urban League and all the civil rights activists who gave their lives in the pursuit of equality and dignity.

I could never really get angry at the old Stepin Fetchits and Aunt Jemimas, for they were uneducated and simply practicing the art of survival.

But I have nothing but contempt for people like Williams and his collaboration with the conservatives. I believe that his actions comfort and aid the racists who, in the name of conservative reform, are taking food out of the mouths of black babies and consigning countless black youths to joblessness.

Jordan is a Plain Dealer reporter.

THE PLAIN DEALER, WEDNESDAY, OCTOBER 12, 1983

Source: George E. Jordan, "Williams speaks for the oppressors," *The Plain Dealer*, October 12, 1983.

Plain Dealer. It was their impression that I wanted to complain about Jordan's attack article.

The editors did most of the talking. They told me that while Jordan's language was harsh, he was well within his rights to call matters as he saw them. The newspaper would not discipline him.

After about fifteen minutes, the editors began to thank me for bringing the matter to their attention—the kind of polite talk that people use to say that the meeting is over. At that point, I asked the editors and executives whether their toleration of Jordan's attack extended to toleration of plagiarism as well; I distributed copies of Jordan's attack on me and Carl Rowan's attack on Tom Sowell, so they could make a side-by-side comparison.

A silence fell over the group as its members alternately read sections of Rowan's article and Jordan's article. One executive said, "This is bad," and an editor noted that Jordan had simply copied Rowan's article while changing a word or two. Declared another *Plain Dealer* executive, "We're embarrassed."

I then proposed that under three conditions, I'd forget the entire matter. First, they fire George Jordan; second, they send me an official letter of apology; and third, they give me space on their editorial page to respond to Jordan's remarks. They didn't accede to my demands.

Instead, *The New York Times* of December 15, 1983, carried the following story:

Plagiarism by Reporter Leads to a Suspension

A reporter for *The Plain Dealer* was reprimanded and suspended for three days for plagiarizing part of a 1981 *Washington Post* column by Carl Rowan, the Cleveland paper said today. The newspaper said George Jordan, a suburban reporter, had "committed a flagrant and inexcusable act of journalistic piracy."

Mr. Jordan's column, published Oct. 12 by the newspaper, included sections that matched the Rowan piece almost word for word. The column by Mr. Jordan was a response to a Sept. 27 speech by Walter E. Williams, a conservative economist.

The Plain Dealer published an editorial addressing the issue today, along with an article in which William F. Buckley Jr., a conservative columnist, criticized the Jordan column. The newspaper said the similarities in the two columns were called to its attention Nov. 16 by Joseph Schwartz, president of Ashland College in Ohio, and that Mr. Jordan was disciplined the next day.

Mr. Rowan said today that he had seen Mr. Jordan's column. "I told him I was not mad at him," he said in Washington, "but I think he made a serious mistake."

The story in the *Times* was incomplete, failing to mention that it was I, accompanied by Dr. Schwartz, who informed *The Plain Dealer* management about the plagiarism. Moreover, the timing of *The Plain Dealer*'s owning up to the plagiarism suggests that the paper was forced into doing so because William Buckley, one of their nationally syndicated columnists, wrote about the matter on the same day. It was obvious, from the mild punishment George Jordan received—a reprimand and a three-day suspension—that *The Plain Dealer* didn't take plagiarism seriously. Of course, it might be that they did take it seriously, but only when whites did the plagiarizing.*

---

* See page 120 for additional news reports on the plagiarism episode.

Conservative scholar victimized by PD reporter, plagiarism

By William F. Buckley Jr.

If you are interested in victimology and want to take a day off from the theme of how President Reagan has victimized women, blacks, Hispanics, old people, invalids and students, give a thought for a moment to the difficulties minority scholars have who, pursuing their researches, reach conclusions different from those peddled by ideological orthodoxy.

They have a hard time. Inevitably they are likened to Uncle Tom. They often are treated with the tacit disdain meted out in many liberal arts faculties toward believing Christians and people suspected of being secretly pro-Reagan (explicit pro-Reaganites are led quietly away to rest homes).

In fact, the anxiety by many blacks to derogate conservative black scholars is so pronounced that assembly-line techniques are being invented. Call this, if you like, supply-side denunciation. I will give you an example.

On Oct. 12, 1983, George E. Jordan, a black journalist, published a column in The Cleveland Plain Dealer. It was entitled, "Williams speaks for the oppressors."

Now I have in my hands, as Joe McCarthy used to say, a photostatic copy of another column, one that appeared almost exactly two years earlier (Sept. 29, 1981) in the Washington Post, by Carl Rowan, another black journalist.

Here are the first two sentences of what Jordan, identified at the end of the column as "a Plain Dealer reporter," wrote: "At times I wish the Lord would deliver me back to the days of Stepin Fetchit, Aunt Jemima and Uncle Tom. The old-style black, illiterate 'handkerchief beads' were an embarrassment, but they were harmless in comparison to 'educated' blacks like economist Walter E. Williams, a darling of the far right."

Here are the first two sentences of what Carl Rowan wrote two years earlier: "There are times when I want to ask the Lord to deliver us back to the days of Stepin Fetchit, Aunt Jemima and Uncle Tom. The old-style black, illiterate, obsequious 'handkerchief heads' were an embarrassment, but they were harmless compared with the 'educated' blacks who are now the darlings of the far right."

The only contribution made by The Plain Dealer's Jordan was to insert "like economist Walter E. Williams." This he needed to do for

so simple a reason as that Rowan, in his column, was denouncing not Walter Williams, but his brother, the distinguished black economist and sociologist, Thomas Sowell.

Now we must not conclude that Jordan is entirely incapable of originality, that he relies exclusively on plagiarizing the work of others. Listen to how the two men ended their columns:

Rowan on Sowell, 1981: "I could never get really angry at the old Stepin Fetchits and Aunt Jemimas. They were poorly educated, and just practicing the art of survival. But I have only contempt for today's butter-tongued apologists for those who are the new oppressors of America's down-and-out people."

Jordan on Williams, 1983: "I could never really get angry at the old Stepin Fetchits and Aunt Jemimas, for they were uneducated and simply practicing the art of survival. But I have nothing but contempt for people like Williams and his collaboration with the conservatives. I believe that his actions comfort and aid the racists who, in the name of conservative reform, are taking food out of the mouths of black babies and consigning countless black youths to joblessness."

Both Williams and Sowell, perhaps because they are better educated than Jordan and Rowan, feel nothing but contempt for argumentation carried on at the level practiced by Jordan and Rowan. I do not believe that any public policies ever espoused by Williams have ever taken food out of the mouths of black babies, but Jordan has sure taken a lot of words out of the mouth of a black grown-up.

It is a pity that some black spokesmen wish to give out the impression that all dissenters are secret members of the Ku Klux Klan. All the more so since the researches of such scholars as Williams and Sowell are of major relevance to exactly the conditions deplored by such as Jordan and Rowan. Which reminds me, since they write exactly the same thing, right down to the identical words, shouldn't they write joint columns? That way, each could have alternate days off.

Buckley, a columnist for the Universal Press Syndicate, is editor of the National Review. Political columnist Brent Larkin, whose column usually is printed in this space, is on vacation.

Source: William F. Buckley Jr., "Conservative scholar victimized by PD reporter, plagiarism," *The Plain Dealer* (1983).

During this period, other attacks took place; for example, one by former NAACP Executive Director Benjamin Hooks called black conservatives, "a new breed of Uncle Tom [and] some of the biggest liars the world ever saw." Carl Rowan also wrote that Sowell and I were "supplicants" for largess from the Reagan administration. Neither Sowell nor I worked for the administration, nor did we receive any money from or through it.

At Work and at Leisure in South Africa

During the 1980s, I sometimes lectured on South Africa. My campus receptions varied from hospitable to hostile. During that period, the sanctions movement had taken off in the United States and around the world. I had the opportunity to visit South Africa several times, first in 1979, at the invitation of the then-director of the country's Free Market Foundation. During my visits, I delivered lectures to major groups—Afrikaners, British, blacks, colored, and Indian.

Discussing apartheid, in both South Africa and the United States, I'd ask why racial laws existed in South Africa? I'd explain that whenever you see one on the books, the most obvious reason is because in its absence not everyone would behave according to the specifications of the law. Thus, the fact that South Africa had numerous discriminatory laws—such as those specifying "job reservation," which prohibited blacks from becoming engine drivers, elevator operators, and so forth—suggested that in absence of these laws, they would be hired for such positions.

Free markets exact a cost for discrimination, and for that reason, one would expect less of it. Achieving the level of racial discrimination that one saw in South Africa required the subversion of free-market forces through legal and political means.

The true irony in South Africa is that groups like the African National Congress, along with white liberals who wanted to help blacks, were calling for socialism. How blacks were seduced into thinking that socialism would be their salvation was impressed upon me during a lecture at the University of Transkei, when a black institution had set up during the apartheid era in the Xhosa homeland of the same name. My lecture had nothing to do with racial issues or apartheid; it was on industrial organization. During the ensuing question and answer session, however, one of the students arose to tell me that he was against capitalism and for socialism. Quite a few others demonstrated their approval through polite applause.

I decided to ask the student a few questions. "Do you think you ought to have the right to live wherever you please?" Yes, he said. "And be able to work for whoever is willing to hire you? Do you think you ought to be served in restaurants and hotels?" He again said yes.

I explained to the class that laissez-faire capitalism, or what some people call free markets, is consistent with the choice preferences demonstrated by the student's answers to my questions. By contrast, socialism is defined as government ownership and/or control over the means of production. I told the students that South Africa's socialism, not capitalism, has been the major socioeconomic barrier for blacks, serving as a tool to benefit white South Africans at the expense of their black fellow countrymen. What blacks needed, I said, was a free-market economic system: the right to work for whomever they please; the right to buy and sell whatever they want from and to anyone they chose.

When I expressed those ideas to some black South African leaders, I often met a hostile reception. Not surprisingly, people who are wedded to the idea that socialism is the cure for the ills of mankind don't like any argument that socialism is the villain of the piece.

Nor was my calling South Africa a socialist nation warmly accepted among white citizens, those who identified themselves as either anti-apartheid white liberals or pro-apartheid Afrikaners. Ultimately, my ideas would lead to a book; published in 1989, it bore the suitable title of *South Africa's War against Capitalism.*

I enjoyed all of my trips to South Africa. On three of them, I was accompanied by Connie and Devyn, and our hosts treated us royally. We had no problems with apartheid, because as Leon Louw put it, the necessary paperwork was done to make us "honorary white people." That meant we stayed at such stately hotels as the Sunnyside Park and Carleton during shorter visits, and enjoyed a lovely apartment in a Johannesburg high-rise and a Mercedes-Benz during our 1980 three-month stint. Just about every day, we were wined, dined, and entertained. There was so

My father and Devyn.

much hospitality that Connie and I often looked forward to quiet evenings alone with our daughter.

Devyn, who was five years old at the time, attended Roedean, a prestigious traditional-British girls' school in the Parktown section of Johannesburg. Initially, she was placed in "grade naught" (kindergarten). The teachers were impressed by Devyn's performance. She was already reading and had nearly perfect diction. On top of that, she was showing other children how to read and explaining pictures to them. About a week or so after school started, the headmistress informed us that Devyn would be promoted to Grade 1. Regardless of what Roedean teachers and students thought about the intelligence of blacks, they were forced to confront the fact that there was at least one black youngster who was as smart or smarter than the whites of her own age.

Devyn was the only black girl in Roedean. Silvie Muholland, wife of the *Financial Mail*'s editor, Stephen Mulholland, might have pulled some strings to have her enrolled there. After all, apartheid law prohibited blacks from attending school with whites. But the key factor was

Strategizing in a 1986 chess game with Devyn, who looks less uncertain than I do.

probably that "honorary white person" designation that was bestowed on us (and that Leon Louw joked so much about). Devyn loved Roedean, and we loved it for her; the teachers and other students were quite receptive and friendly. Everything at the school was rather formal in the British tradition, including curtsies to the headmistress by the female students as they were dismissed at the end of the day. Connie participated in school activities and became friends with a few of the parents.

Leon Louw kept me quite busy giving lectures to various groups throughout the country. What surprised me most initially was the friendliness of South Africans, white as well as black. I had an office at Rands-Afrikaans University, where most of the students and professors were Afrikaners. There might have been a few British, but no blacks. Through my conversations there and elsewhere, I began to gain an understanding of, though not necessarily sympathy for, Afrikaner feelings toward black South Africans.

Afrikaners argued that comparisons between American blacks and those of South Africa were fallacious. They said American blacks were essentially Europeans in terms of culture and values, while South African blacks were Third World people with non-European cultures and values. They maintained that a more appropriate comparison would be between American Indians and South African blacks, both of whom differ culturally from Europeans. Moreover, they pointed to overt American racism, brutality, and lynchings that were never a significant factor in South Africa. Afrikaners also cited what they saw as their general humaneness toward their native peoples, again compared to the comparable Americans' situation.

"We," said South African whites, "seek to separate instead of exterminate." In other words, they argued that Americans killed off much of their potential problems while South African whites tried to set up "homelands"—separate living areas for their native population.

Another thing that impressed me was the relatively poor economic training of South African professors at both black and white universities, particularly at Afrikaner institutions such as Stellenbosh and Potchefstroom. The only institutions I found comparable to those in the United States in that respect were Witswatersrand in Johannesburg, Natal in Durban, and Capetown University.

Our three-month stay in South Africa was both enlightening and enjoyable, though somewhat frustrating in terms of the debate over how South Africans saw their problems and the solutions to them. Two days before we were to depart, I was invited to address the Barclays Bank Women's Executive Committee. It was a luncheon attended by several hundred people from all of the country's major groups.

In the first few sentences of my address, I voiced my disappointment in South African society. I told the audience that I believed that South Africans deserved one another, because it was my observation that very few South Africans were for true liberty. Blacks, who've been the chief victims of an unjust system, as demonstrated elsewhere in post-colonial Africa, simply wanted to change the color of the dictator. Afrikaners wanted to maintain some version of the status quo. Liberal whites, for the most part British, wanted an "enlightened" apartheid in the form of racial preferences and quotas and creating special privileges for non-whites.

My last visit to South Africa came in 1989, in conjunction with the publication of *South Africa's War against Capitalism*. Nelson Mandela was about to be released from prison, and everyone expected that apartheid was seeing its last days. In my lectures, I stressed that the most important issue for black South Africans wasn't ending apartheid but figuring out what was going to replace it. I cautioned that elsewhere on the continent, when European colonialism came to an end, people didn't pay a lot of attention to what was going to replace colonialism. Now, in many of those countries, black dictatorships have imposed a system of horrors on their people that would have been unthinkable to their European colonial masters.

As evidence, I mentioned the genocidal atrocities in Uganda, Burundi, Rwanda, Nigeria, and elsewhere that have snuffed out millions of lives. I argued that in some countries, if you asked a black person who lived under both colonial and black rule which was better for him, he'd say that, in terms of material well-being and personal liberty, he preferred colonial. Wouldn't it be a supreme tragedy for black South Africans, I asked, if a time came where a black South African could say that he was better off under apartheid?

During the 1980s, there were numerous demonstrations and calls for economic sanctions against, and disinvestment in, South Africa as punishment for its apartheid policy. During this period, I gave numerous lectures on American college campuses, presented congressional testimony, and took part in the sanctions and disinvestment debate through my columns and radio-TV appearances.

One memorable lecture, which highlights some of the moral posturing over the debate, led to my physician asking me to discuss the issue with his church members. He said that the question of whether the church should keep or get rid of shares in companies that did business in South Africa was tearing the church apart. I gave my standard lecture highlighting some of the complexities and difficulties the nation faced. During the question and answer period, one of the church elders said he considered it a sin for the church to hold shares of a company operating in a country that treated its black population so badly.

"What," I replied, "would you propose doing with those shares?" His response: instruct the church's broker to sell them. "And just how Christian would it be," I responded, "for the church, in order to wipe itself clean of this 'sin,' to cause another person or institution to commit the same sin by *buying* those stocks?"

There was, I suggested, another way the church could free itself from the ownership of what he regarded as morally tainted property. The room in which I was addressing the congregation contained a fireplace with a toasty blaze. Why not simply toss the shares into it? Told that such a solution was impractical, I politely replied, "What you really mean is that when moral posturing entails a financial cost, you're less willing to engage in it."

I made my summary point: getting rid of their shares of U.S. companies doing business in South Africa wouldn't do a darn thing to assist South African blacks; all it would do is make some of the church members feel better.

Traveling the World

In 1978, I was invited to participate in the Hong Kong, Tokyo, and Taiwan joint meetings of the Mont Pelerin Society. The society was formed in 1947 by Friedrich von Hayek, Milton Friedman, and 34 other scholars, mostly economists but historians and philosophers as well. In the post-World War II era, socialism was on the ascendency and the values of limited government and personal liberty in decline. These scholars wanted to form an organization that would meet occasionally to deliver papers on issues dealing with free markets and liberty.

Today the Mont Pelerin Society has more than 500 members from forty nations, and holds general and regional meetings all over the world. The highly distinguished membership has included eight Nobel Laureates. The name Mont Pelerin was chosen after the place of the first meeting, on Lac Leman in Switzerland.

My membership has enabled me to exchange points of view with many individuals and learn many cultures. In fact, it was at the Hong

Kong meetings that I met Leon Louw, which led to my several invitations to South Africa. Membership has also made it possible for my family and me to attend meetings in Cambridge, West Berlin, Santiago, Vancouver, Rio de Janeiro, Guatemala, Cancún, Stockholm, St. Vincent, Italy, and elsewhere. As a result, we have friends and colleagues worldwide.

The Mont Pelerin Society has no political agenda and holds no press conferences. That doesn't mean that particular members are not involved politically in their own countries. In fact, some of the members have been prominent government officials: Chancellor Ludwig Erhard of then-West Germany, President Luigi Einaudi of Italy, Chairman Arthur Burns of the U.S. Federal Reserve board of governors, and Prime Minister Vaclav Klaus of the Czech Republic.

Dealing with Congress and the White House

During the Reagan years, I continued to receive invitations to give testimony before both the House of Representatives and the Senate. Anyone who attends hearings or witnesses them on C-SPAN can see how most people who are called to testify are deferential and even obsequious. Not I. It has always been my opinion that, save for a precious few congressmen, these people are not deserving of the honor and respect they receive. I regard most of them, save a handful or so, as enemies of both the Constitution and the moral precepts of our Founding Fathers—a regular theme of my nationally syndicated columns.

Several of my appearances before Congress didn't turn out to be pleasant. In April 1983, when I testified before the House Select Committee on Children, Youth, and Families, Representative Mickey Leland disagreed with my discussion of the negative effects that government programs have on minorities. At one point, during a rancorous exchange, I said that congressmen use their agents at the Internal Revenue Service to confiscate the property of one American to give to another American. Leland responded that he was "totally disoriented" by my remarks. Congress, he declared, "has to come to the aid of those people who cannot do for themselves. That is the only way that blacks and Hispanics and women have been able to afford opportunities in this country to date."

I told the congressman that he was playing games with words: "What you are describing is charity, and charity is an improper description for a government activity." I added that the IRS does not ask me to give it money; it *demands* money. A frustrated and angry Mickey Leland bellowed, "I never thought I would say this, but thank God for the IRS!"

In April 1981, I was asked to give testimony before the Senate Labor Committee on the Davis-Bacon Act. During Ray Marshall's term as secretary of labor in the Carter administration, he had testified before the corresponding House sub-committee that Davis-Bacon did not have discriminatory effects on non-union workers and blacks. The fact, however, is that the act was racially motivated law, and it sought to prevent black construction workers from competing with their white counterparts.

Consider the following samples of the 1931 testimony in support of the legislation: Representative Clayton Allgood of Alabama said, "Reference has been made to a contractor from Alabama who went to New York with bootleg labor. This is a fact. That contractor has cheap colored labor that he transports, and he puts them in cabins, and it is labor of that sort that is in competition with white labor throughout the country. This bill has merit, and with the extensive building program now being entered into, it is very important that we enact this measure."[*] Representative John J. Cochran of Missouri echoed similar sentiments, saying that he had "received numerous complaints in recent months about Southern contractors employing low-paid colored mechanics getting work and bringing the employees from the South."[†] William Green, president of the AFL, made the union's position clear: "[C]olored labor is being sought to demoralize wage rates [in Tennessee]."[‡]

I photocopied a few pages from Ray Marshall's labor-economics textbook, written when he was a professor at the University of Texas, and gave them to committee members. In his book, Marshall said that the Davis-Bacon Act had been useful to the building trades in preventing

---

[*] Cong. Rec. H6, 71st Cong., 3rd sess. (1931): 513.

[†] House Committee on Labor, *Hearings on H.R. 7995 & H.R. 9232*, 71st Cong., 2nd sess. (1930): 26–27.

[‡] Senate Committee on Manufactures, *Hearings S.5904*, 71st Cong., 3rd sess. (1931): 10.

non-union wage competition. To the extent that most black construction workers were non-union, it was racially discriminatory.

Senator Orrin Hatch asked me whether I thought the act's discriminatory effects have changed between Marshall's writing of his textbook and his testimony before the House Labor Subcommittee that contradicted the book. I responded, "I do not think the conditions have changed since the secretary wrote his book. I think what happened is that his *position* changed, because he got a new job and had to do the bidding of his sponsors." Senator Hatch replied, "I see. It is surprising how closely you and I think."

In December 1981, Hatch invited me to another hearing on Davis-Bacon. I began my testimony by telling the senators about what I saw as the major problem in our nation: "You men win your way into office and retain that office essentially by promising some Americans that you will give them the fruits of another man's labor. You also win office by promising one group of Americans that they will be given a right or privilege that will be denied other Americans."

Before I could get into the meat of my remarks, about the specific effects of the Davis-Bacon Act, Hatch interrupted. "Wait a minute, Walter," he said. "Are you saying for a minute here that us wonderful senators and congressmen love to take taxpayers' money and go out and give it away so that we can buy votes with it?"

I said, "Yes, I am."

"You are?" the senator asked again.

"Yes, I am."

"Well," Hatch said, "I agree with you. As a matter of fact, that may be one reason why it is so difficult for President Reagan to balance the budget—isn't it?" At that point, Senator Ted Kennedy walked out of the hearings.

Consorting with the Reagan Administration

I had a minor government involvement during the early stages of the Reagan presidency. In 1980, I accepted an unpaid position on the White

House transition team at the U.S. Department of Labor. As I understood them, my duties included acquiring information about a particular agency, so as to be able to brief the new president and his staff on pending legal or regulatory matters and perhaps make some recommendations. Some members of the department's transition team were meeting with Washington lobbyists and department employees who were jockeying for positions in the new administration. I thought that was improper, so I resigned—before noon on my first day.

Raymond Donovan, who became Reagan's secretary of labor, invited me to have lunch with him to discuss the possibility of my becoming deputy secretary. As a matter of courtesy, I accepted the invitation, though I had no real intention of taking the position if it were offered. The very next day, I received a call from Professor Friedman saying that he had heard I was being considered for the position with the Department of Labor. He could well understand how flattered I'd be by such an offer, but he admonished me not to accept it.

Friedman explained: "They'll do one of two things to you—embarrass you or compromise your principles. You're far too valuable to the liberty movement to allow either to happen." His advice sealed my decision.

I called Ray Donovan and told him that I doubted I'd win confirmation in the first place and that if I did accept any high-level administration position, the president would wind up having to call a news conference once a week to explain to the nation why he had appointed this crazy-ass man who insisted on talking about liberty in America. I also explained that I wasn't sure whether I could be a team player, as opposed to a loose cannon: "Joining an administration is very much like joining an orchestra. If you're going to join an orchestra, you ought to agree to pay attention to the maestro, but I'm the kind of guy who often likes to fiddle his own tune."

Although I didn't join the administration, I participated in "brown bag" working lunches and other meetings at the White House with the presidential staff, and on a couple of occasions with the president and vice president themselves. While invited several times to state dinners, I attended only one: for the president of Uruguay. I went to that one under a threat from Mrs. Williams, who had seen me turn down several previous invitations and wanted us to attend at least one such function. Surprisingly, I had the guest-of-honor seat at President Reagan's left, and we had a lively discussion on several public-policy matters. Connie and I had a fine evening, capped off, during the drive home, by her caustic comments on the intelligence I had displayed in not accepting previous state-dinner invitations.

Coming on with a Rush

During the late '70s and '80s, I gained considerable national exposure through debates, lectures, television interviews, and hundreds of radio appearances. I took part in one of the debate segments of Friedman's *Free to Choose* series as well as the following programs: WQLN's *Star Spangled Spenders*; the WTBS Debate Series called *Counterpoint*; William F. Buckley's *Firing Line*; ABC's *Nightline*; CBS's *Nightwatch*; *Face the Nation*; *Crossfire*; *The MacNeil/Lehrer NewsHour*; CNN's *Larry King Show*; various C-SPAN shows; and ABC's *Inside Story*. I also provided commentaries for the PBS *Nightly Business Report*.

All of that was in addition to my weekly nationally syndicated column. My national exposure accelerated during the 1990s. In 1992, James Golden, who at the time was Rush Limbaugh's call screener, asked me whether Representative Robert Dornan, a regular substitute host on the show, could interview me by telephone. I agreed. Typically, when I'm interviewed, I virtually take over the show, asking both the host and callers questions. The Dornan "Q & A" went very well.

Golden called again soon thereafter: Would I be interested in guest hosting for Limbaugh when he went out of town? "Yes," I said, "but I want to speak to Rush first." I wanted to be sure that I wasn't being used in a fashion contrary to his wishes and best interests. Rush assured me that everything was okay with him. When I confessed that I'd never hosted a show before, he told me not to worry and said that with the help of his staff, I would do fine.

In October 1992, I hosted Rush's show for the very first time, and I've occasionally played that role ever since. It has always been a delight to fill in for Rush Limbaugh. I call the show my big classroom, an opportunity to talk to millions upon millions of listeners. Taken together, my public "appearances"—radio and television interviews and the nationally syndicated column—have been a tremendous learning experience. Listeners and readers have often either called in or written to me to ask, "Have you thought of it this way?" or to say, "When I was young, this happened. . . ." or "An example of what you were saying is. . . ." All of that feedback, both positive and negative, has vastly enriched my knowledge and understanding, making me a better-informed person and commentator.

Limbaugh's program is the most popular talk-radio show in U.S. history, carried on 622 broadcast stations plus satellite outlets. My appearances as substitute host have therefore increased both the demand for my speaking services and the honoraria connected with them. I have received several inquiries about having my own show. I've turned them all down, preferring to focus on my first love, teaching.

Becoming a Department Chairman

In 1995, several of my George Mason colleagues asked me about accepting the chairmanship of the economics department. My initial response was a hearty laugh. An administrative position was the last thing that would have crossed my mind, and I didn't take their suggestion seriously. After the question was posed several more times, I decided to think more seriously about the position. The first person I consulted, expecting support for my inclination not to accept it, was Thomas Sowell.

"Tom," I said, "if you heard that Walter accepted the chairmanship of George Mason's economics department, would you conclude that he's finally lost it?" I was truly surprised by Tom's response. He asked me how long had I been teaching at George Mason. When I said, "almost fifteen years," he replied, "Then it's probably your turn." Except for a short stint as project director at the Urban Institute, he himself has spent his career avoiding anything of an administrative nature. So I was counting on him for a good argument to present to my colleagues by way of declining to be a candidate. But given Tom's response and their considerable cajoling,

I indicated my willingness to take on the job, and received a unanimous vote from the faculty.

Our department was in pretty bad shape in a fairly hostile university environment. In 1986, when James Buchanan, my colleague and former mentor at UCLA, won the Nobel Prize, George Mason's economics faculty numbered twenty-six. In 1995, when I assumed the chairmanship, there were twenty. The administration had denied the previous department chairman, Richard Wagner, the opportunity to fill positions vacated by faculty who either resigned or took different positions within the university.

Early in my term as chairman, I tried everything possible to persuade the dean of the College of Arts and Sciences, at that time David Potter, to authorize new positions to replace the lost faculty members. Dr. Potter was much more interested in reallocating resources to create what is called New Century College. The kind of courses, with little or no academic content, taught within the college included: HIV/AIDS Awareness, Habitat for Humanity, Construct of Difference: Race, Class & Gender, and, more recently, Beats, Rhymes and Culture, a course that examines the history of hip-hop music. Dean Potter had perfected the practice of moving resources from high-value uses to low-value uses.

Hostility toward our department also emanated from some other quarters on campus. Why? We had no liberal economists. Most of our department faculty would place themselves in the conservative, libertarian, or free-market camps. As is generally the case at American universities, the faculty at George Mason is predominantly liberal. The important distinction between that institution and, say, the University of Massachusetts or University of California/Berkeley is that our campus liberals aren't nearly as extreme and are generally polite professionals. Aside from ideological differences between our department and the rest of the university, there was resentment over the fact that economics professors earned salaries considerably higher than many other arts and sciences faculty members. That reflected no bias in favor of economists; it was simply the reality of the academic marketplace for them compared to that for other social scientists.

In addition, the administration took a couple of nasty actions with regard to the economics department. It appropriated our conference room without my consent, even without consultation. It also threatened to take the offices of some of our senior faculty members. That happened after a fairly hostile telephone conversation between the associate dean and me, a conversation I ended by abruptly hanging up. Administrative hostility toward me also gave a small faction in our department an opportunity to create sympathy for the faction's attempt to relocate the graduate studies portion of our program. Fortunately, those efforts failed.

In the face of such administrative hostility, I decided that the only way to improve and build the economics department was to "privatize" it. That is, I would seek external funding to improve and add resources. I was the first economics department chairman to attempt that, and my efforts proved successful. Generous grants from foundations and private individuals allowed me to do some things that weren't done previously, among them, offer several visiting professorships, purchase equipment, negotiate with the administration to pay part of the salaries for additional faculty, and underwrite expenses such as recruitment costs and moving costs for new faculty, student/faculty travel to professional meetings, faculty summer-research stipends, graduate student fellowships, and undergraduate student awards.

It's customary for department chairmen to seek funds from the dean's office for travel, equipment, and other budget items. During my entire term as department chairman, however, I never sought departmental funds from any other university official and raised well over a million dollars through my personal contacts. I did demand that I/we be left alone.

A godsend for our department was the appointments then-Virginia Governor James Gilmore made to George Mason's Board of Visitors (university trustees). They included former U.S. Attorney General Ed Meese; Ed Feulner, president of the Heritage Foundation; Richard Fink, former faculty member and board member of Koch Industries; James Miller, former director of the federal Office of Management and Budget; and Manuel Johnson, former vice chairman of the Federal Reserve board.

These men all took an interest in the university and had little sympathy for the politically correct nonsense countenanced, if not encouraged, on many university campuses these days. In addition, at this juncture, I knew all of them well. Though I am not privy to what they said or did about the hostility directed at our department, the university's behavior toward us changed in a favorable direction.

When Daniele Struppa became dean of the College of Arts and Sciences at about the same time, his predecessor, David Potter, who was being promoted to provost, had been briefed that I was a troublemaker. Not surprisingly, therefore, toward the end of my first term as department chairman, Dr. Struppa asked me whether I would be standing for re-election. When I told him yes, he suggested that I not do so, explaining that the real opposition to me came from Alan Merten, George Mason's president. I replied that there was too much dishonesty at the university and that I wasn't going to allow him to do the dirty work for the president.

Department faculty members vote to elect their chairman, with the president then accepting or rejecting it. I told Struppa that I would allow my colleagues to elect me. If Alan Merten didn't approve, he could reject their decision. I was voted into "office" for a second term, and Merten didn't counter the vote. If he had done so, I imagine he'd have had a lot of explaining to do to the Board of Visitors, especially given their knowledge of the conflict between me and the administration.

Daniele Struppa, a mathematician by training, was the first scholar who served as dean of the College of Arts and Sciences. His predecessors were little more than political hacks with few academic credentials. His scholarly training eventually led him to appreciate my efforts to build a strong academic department. Years later, he told me that he had been completely misled about me and the economics department. He acknowledged that the attacks on me and our department were politically inspired. At the end of my term as chairman, he told a large group gathered to honor my achievements that I had built the strongest department among the almost two dozen in the college.

Indeed, our economics faculty boasted two Nobel Laureates, James Buchanan and Vernon Smith; the latter was hired during my last year as

Devyn and Clarence, two of the toasters at a 2003 tribute to me by my George Mason University colleagues.

chairman, and a year after that, he won the award. In addition, we have a number of young scholars who show great promise for the future. Today, Daniele and I are good friends and associates who dine together now and then and share confidences. I could not have crafted our departmental achievements without the assistance of several hardworking senior colleagues and the generous philanthropic contributions from numerous individuals and such foundations as John M. Olin, Koch, Scaife, and Eli Lilly.

In 2001, I stepped down as chairman after my colleagues and I hired Dr. Donald Boudreaux as my successor. Leaving that position was a welcome relief to me. The best description I can give for the job is that it's akin to herding cats—or, perhaps worse, mules: leading faculty members who have their own goals and agendas, but with no stout stick, only a carrot, in hand.

With no more administrative responsibilities, I have settled easily back into teaching. The Olin foundation's generous funding has provided me with the John M. Olin Distinguished Professorship chair, covering most of my salary. As a result, I teach only one class a semester: in the fall, our graduate course in microeconomics theory; in the spring, an intermediate course on the same subject.

At the age of seventy-four, one begins to wind up one's life. I hope that my last days are spent doing exactly what I'm doing as I complete this autobiography: teaching, writing, and making occasional radio-TV appearances.

CHAPTER SEVEN

Afterthoughts

MY AGE—SEVENTY-FOUR at this writing—affords insights unavailable to those with fewer years. It is particularly helpful in evaluating some of today's racial dogma.

Part of that dogma has to do with what I call the civil rights vision of race, whose central premise is that statistical disparities in income, education, and other socioeconomic variables are moral injustices caused by society. Underlying the premise are several assumptions taken to be axiomatic and hence beyond question: for example, that racial discrimination leads to adverse effects on the achievement of those discriminated against and that progress can't be made until discrimination is eliminated.

There's no question that my youthful years saw a level of racial discrimination unknown today. In assessing its effects, one must ask questions: how much of what we see can be explained by discrimination alone? How much of a barrier to self-improvement is discrimination? What kinds of tools are in the ready grasp of those subjected to it? Surely one doesn't want to sit around waiting for the end to discrimination.

At a very early age, my mother introduced my sister and me to the Philadelphia public library. When we moved to North Philadelphia, we spent many a Saturday or Sunday morning at the city's main library. My mother also introduced us to the Philadelphia Museum of Art and the Franklin Institute, with its scientific exhibits. Since the art museum was close to the library, our Saturday or Sunday outing often included a visit there or to the city's aquarium. We seldom actually visited the Franklin Institute, because it charged a fee for admission. During the 1980s, I repeated this Saturday-Sunday pattern with my own daughter, frequently taking her to the institute.

In the '80s as well as the '60s, I recall seeing few other black people at these places; at the institute, most of the time, Devyn and I were the only blacks present. Yet the educational and cultural enrichment that can be gained by exposing one's children to museums and libraries is beyond the capacity of racists to deny. Another part of my upbringing, which they also can't deny, was my mother's insistence, not always successful, that we do our homework and behave in school.

Prevailing racial dogma asserts that black role models in teaching are necessary to raise black achievement, instill pride, and offset the effects of our legacy of slavery and subsequent discrimination. This brand of dogma comes with a self-serving component that in the past has supported calls for racial preferences in hiring at primary, secondary, and university levels of education.

Attending predominantly black junior high and high schools, and graduating from the latter in 1954, I recall having no more than two, possibly three, black teachers; that was true of my primary education as well. The photograph of my 1950 junior high graduating class of 275 students, 18 of whom were white, shows no black school administrators; the principals and vice principals, and all but one of the teachers, are white. Nonetheless, many of my classmates, who grew up in the Richard Allen housing project and with whom I've kept up over the years, managed to become middle-class adults; and one, Bill Cosby, became a multi-millionaire. Our role models were primarily our parents and family; any teachers who also served in that role were white, not black.

Every couple of years, former Richard Allen residents hold a reunion. When I've attended, I've asked some of my friends and ex-schoolmates whether they recall any of our peers who couldn't read and write well enough to fill out a job application or who spoke the poor language that's often heard today among black youngsters. The answer is they don't remember anyone doing either.

Yet in 2005, at my high school alma mater, Benjamin Franklin, only 4 percent of eleventh-grade students scored "proficient" and above in reading, 12 percent in writing, and 1 percent in math. Today's Philadelphia school system includes a high percentage of black teachers and black administrators, but academic achievement is a shadow of what it was yesteryear. If the dogma about role models had any substance, the opposite should be the case.

It's not just blacks to whom the role-model dogma doesn't apply. Japanese-Americans and Chinese-Americans, as a group, score near or at the top in most tests of academic achievement. Historically, however, those children have been taught by white teachers.

By any income measure, my family was poor. But we didn't see ourselves as poor. We always had a roof over our heads and never missed a meal. Through frugality, or as my mother called it, "pinching pennies," we were even able to enjoy trips to New York, Atlantic City, and amusement parks. And if materially poor, we were spiritually rich. My grandmother used to preach, "You don't have to be rich to be clean." Mom taught us that although we had a beer pocketbook, we had champagne tastes. Nowadays, very few blacks suffer yesteryear's material poverty, but many lack its spiritual wealth.

Recalling some of the highlights and turning points in my life has helped me recognize several aspects of my own success in the context of the human condition. One of those surely is this: being the first in my entire family's history to graduate even from high school—then go on to college, earn a doctorate, and register many other achievements—is phenomenal progress for anyone of any race, but even more impressive for a black person from a poor family who was born in 1936, during a period of racial discrimination, deep economic depression, and therefore relatively few opportunities.

Yet no one who has gone from the bottom to the top has done so on his own. In my life there were known, and possibly unknown, helpers along the way. There was also a measure of sheer luck—being at the right place, or even the wrong place, at the right time. Looking back, I think about specific events and speculate on alternative outcomes. Among them: suppose I had never encountered tough primary and secondary school teachers like Mrs. Viola Meekins and Dr. Martin Rosenberg, who didn't give a damn about my self-esteem. Where would I be now?

Suppose I hadn't gotten a job driving a taxi for Yellow Cab. More than likely, I would have never met Connie. Would another marriage partner been as faithful and supportive, and would she have shared my vision? Of course, it's impossible to tell, but I'm guessing the answer is no.

There was Professor Arthur Kirsch, who was not only a mentor but was also instrumental, later on, in helping me land my first full-time teaching appointment. And there was my father's fourth wife, who encouraged me to participate in her sorority's Seagram's Gin scholarship contest; although I didn't win, one of the judges encouraged me to apply to UCLA's graduate school, and that led to my being educated by some of the brightest minds in economics.

I've benefited from receiving virtually all of my education before it became fashionable for white people to like black people. The result: whatever grades I received were earned, as opposed to given. Teachers provided an honest assessment of my learning. They weren't reluctant to tell me, "Williams, that's just plain nonsense." Or, as Professor Axel Leijonhufvud said, after I and ten others flunked the theory portion of UCLA's PhD preliminary exams, "Williams, your exam was among the worst" (mercifully adding, "but we think you can do better"). Far too many blacks today don't receive honest assessments of their work or abilities, due to a teacher's misguided efforts to compensate for our history of being discriminated against or fear of intimidation by students and accusations of racism.

Since much of what I've achieved has not only been a result of hard work and sacrifice but luck and chance as well, I cannot suggest that the way I've led my life provides a blueprint for upward mobility. The best advice I can offer is that given to me by my stepfather. A lot of life, he used to tell me, is luck and chance, and you never know when the opportunity train is going to come along. He said that if and when it comes, don't be in the position of saying, "Wait! Let me go and pack my bag." Be packed and ready to hop on board.

Finally, so much of what I've accomplished has stemmed from the immeasurable assistance of two ladies in my life. The first is my mother, a determined, disciplined woman who made personal sacrifices as she struggled to raise my sister and me. She was uncompromising in her expectations, and she instilled in us a sense of independence and the desire for a better life. The other lady is my wife, who shared my vision and through diligence, patience, and love managed to polish off many of my rough edges.

◆ ◆ ◆

Index